Two Plays from
the New Russia

Russian Theatre Archive

A series of books edited by John Freedman (Moscow), Leon Gitelman
(St Petersburg) and Anatoly Smeliansky (Moscow)

Two Plays from
the New Russia

Bald/Brunet
by Daniil Gink

and

Nijinsky
by Alexei Burykin

Translated and Edited
by
John Freedman

 harwood academic publishers
Australia • Canada • China • France • Germany • India • Japan
Luxembourg • Malaysia • The Netherlands • Russia • Singapore
Switzerland • Thailand • United Kingdom

Emmaplein 5
1075 AW Amsterdam
The Netherlands

Applications to perform the plays should be addressed to the translator in care of Harwood Academic Publishers.

British Library Cataloguing in Publication Data

Gink, Daniil
  Two Plays from the New Russia: "Bald/Brunet"
  by Daniil Gink and "Nijinsky" by Alexei Burykin. –
  (Russian Theatre Archive, ISSN 1068–9161; Vol. 9)
  I. Title   II. Burykin, Alexei
  III. Freedman, John   IV. Series
  891.724408

  ISBN 3–7186–5780–5 (hardback)
  ISBN 3–7186–5781–3 (paperback)

CONTENTS

INTRODUCTION TO THE SERIES

The Russian Theatre Archive makes available in English the best avant-garde plays from the pre-Revolutionary period to the present day. It features monographs on major playwrights and theatre directors, introductions to previously unknown works, and studies of the main artistic groups and periods.

Plays are presented in performing edition translations, including (where appropriate) musical scores, and instructions for music and dance. Whenever possible the translated texts will be accompanied by videotapes of performances of plays in the original language.

LIST OF PLATES
(Between pp. 44 and 45)

1. Pyotr Mamonov, as the Bald Man, and Denis Burgazliev, as the Brunet, in *Bald/Brunet* at the Stanislavsky Theater, Moscow, 1991. (Photo: Mikhail Guterman)
2. Pyotr Mamonov and Denis Burgazliev performing in *Bald/Brunet* at the Stanislavsky Theater, Moscow, 1991. (Photo: Mikhail Guterman)
3. Lyudmila Lushina, as the Young Woman, and Pyotr Mamonov, as the Bald Man, in *Bald/Brunet* at the Stanislavsky Theater, Moscow, 1991. (Photo: Mikhail Guterman)
4. Denis Burgazliev and Pyotr Mamonov in *Bald/Brunet* at the Stanislavsky Theater, 1991. (Photo: Mikhail Guterman)
5. Pyotr Mamonov in *Bald/Brunet* at the Stanislavsky Theater, Moscow, 1991. (Photo: Mikhail Guterman)
6. Daniil Gink and daughter Masha. (Photo: Victor Bazhenov)
7. Daniil Gink. (Photo: Victor Bazhenov)
8. Oleg Menshikov (Nijinsky) and Alexander Feklistov (the Actor) in the Bogis Agency production of *Nijinsky*, Moscow, 1993. (Photo: the Bogis Agency)
9. Oleg Menshikov as Nijinsky in the Bogis Agency production of *Nijinsky*, Moscow, 1993. (Photo: the Bogis Agency)
10. Alexander Feklistov as the Actor in the Bogis Agency production of *Nijinsky*, Moscow, 1993. (Photo: the Bogis Agency)
11. Alexander Feklistov (the Actor) and Oleg Menshikov (Nijinsky) in the Bogis Agency production of *Nijinsky*, Moscow, 1993. (Photo: the Bogis Agency)
12. Oleg Menshikov (Nijinsky) and Alexander Feklistov (the Actor) in the Bogis Agency production of *Nijinsky*, Moscow, 1993. (Photo: Mikhail Guterman)
13. Alexei Burykin "hangs in the air at the top of a leap" in front of the Alexandrinsky Theater in St. Petersburg. (Photo: Oleg Menshikov)
14. Alexei Burykin in front of a drawing by Vaslav Nijinsky. (Photo: Oleg Menshikov)

INTRODUCTION

The plays comprising this volume, Daniil Gink's *Bald/Brunet* and Alexei Burykin's *Nijinsky*, were the basis for Moscow's two biggest theatrical hits of the early 1990s. They appeared as if out of nowhere at a time when the morale of Russia's theater community was at an all-time low. Many of the established directors were merely repeating themselves, while nearly all of the prolific playwrights of the 1960s, '70s and '80s had fallen silent. New playwrights were having almost no success getting their works performed. Right or wrong, the received opinion was that both playwriting and theater in Russia had died. As often happens, it took the blissful ignorance and fearlessness of inexperience to turn the tide.

When *Bald/Brunet* premiered at the Stanislavsky Theater in December 1991 and became an overnight sensation, Daniil Gink was all of twenty-two years old. Fourteen months later, in the waning days of February 1993, when *Nijinsky* burst onto the scene as the first production of the new Bogis Agency production company, Alexei Burykin was still short of his twenty-fifth birthday. Neither of the young authors had ever written a play before. The amazing success enjoyed by the productions of their plays is eloquent proof that Burykin's Nijinsky knows precisely what he is talking about when he quips that "all experience does is kill a good leap."

Naturally, it would have been too much of a storybook ending had Moscow's well-experienced critics greeted the appearance of the two fledgling dramatists enthusiastically. There is no point in hiding the facts: While the two productions were the proverbial and bona fide talk of the town, and while they performed to nothing but standing-room-only crowds, the critics bucked, balked, sputtered and bickered in regard to the plays themselves. Both authors were said to have been "saved" by great casts. Gink was accused of having written a pale imitation of Eugène Ionesco or Samuel Beckett, while Burykin was either ignored altogether or accused of merely rearranging Nijinsky's diary. But one of the wisest responses came from Viktor Slavkin, the writer whose plays *A Young Man's Grown-Up Daughter* and *Cerceau* provided the material for two of Anatoly Vasilyev's most important productions (1979 and 1985, respectively). Commenting on the state of Russian playwriting in 1994, Slavkin praised *Bald/Brunet* and

Nijinsky as Moscow's two best productions in the last fifteen years, and added pointedly that great productions aren't made from bad plays.[1] Indeed, both of the plays are fresh, original and theatrical. They are laced with the energy and the endlessly attractive boldness of youth, just as they are filled with the kind of wisdom and insight that belies their authors' tender ages.

Even a cursory glance at the texts offers an impressive arsenal of responses to the various criticisms that were aimed at them. Gink's play—a touching, tender exploration of an aging man's reaction to the crass world around him—has almost nothing to do with what we call the theater of the absurd. It is a dreamlike work that often uses stream of consciousness tactics to lay bare the very concrete, very personal experiences and problems of the main character. Meanwhile, aside from quoting some key phrases and using some of the anecdotal material from Nijinsky's diary, Burykin's play is a strikingly imaginative and wholly independent work. It completely transforms the frantic, feverish atmosphere of Nijinsky's diary into a sublime state of wonder and discovery. One of the most curious points surrounding the criticism aimed specifically at the plays is that neither of them (like Nijinsky's diary, incidentally) had been published in Russian.[2] One can't help but wonder what the critical hoopla was based on.

Putting *Bald/Brunet* and *Nijinsky* together in one collection reveals some fascinating similarities between them. And the nature of those similarities has much to say about the key problems that were buffeting Russian culture in the early 1990s. Most striking is that both plays depict artists suffering from some sort of schizophrenic disorder. In the case of *Bald/Brunet*, an aging sax player and rhyme scribbler (the Bald Man) is constantly forced to defend himself against the attacks of a corrosive young man (the Brunet) who is probably only a figment of his own imagination or a product of his memory. In *Nijinsky*, the artist is Vaslav Nijinsky, the great Polish-Russian dancer of Sergei Diaghilev's *Ballets Russes* in the early 20th century. Burykin split the historical figure into two characters: Nijinsky, who represents the dancer's intuitive half, and the Actor, who represents his more practical, cerebral half.

It would be folly to suggest that either Gink or Burykin were specifically attempting to create grand metaphors for the crisis in Russian culture, but it

---

[1] The comment was made to me in conversation. Slavkin published an appreciation of *Nijinsky* in "Uletanie geroya" [A Hero's Parting Leap], *Ogonyok*, Nos. 21/22 (1993), 18–19.

[2] Essentially, neither play has been published in any language until now. A German version of *Bald/Brunet* appeared in *Theater Heute*, in 1992, but it was an unauthorized version that used the much-shortened and occasionally altered production text rather than Gink's play. A back-translation of Nijinsky's diary, from the French, appeared in Russian only in 1995.

is hardly a coincidence that each of them found that the dramatic structure of the split personality best expressed their ideas. The great Russian philosopher Nikolai Berdyaev wrote that "Russians are, by their very psychology, inclined to become schismatics."[3] In fact, Russian history might even be described as a series of schisms that at any given time is either in the process of healing or of being aggravated. Certainly, the collapse of the Soviet Union, brought about by the collapse of the philosophy and ideology that sustained it, has reopened many of the wounds that have caused Russia's schisms in the past. *Bald/Brunet* and *Nijinsky*, both in their structures and in the themes that they raise, bear compelling witness to that.

Also very much within the Russian tradition is the deep human sympathy that is sensed in the authors' attitudes to their creations. Both treat characters in states of acute alienation, confusion and frustration, although the resulting plays are seldom bleak or cruel. The worlds of the works may be largely hostile and deceptive, but they still retain the capacity to offer moments of genuine, meaningful solace. In the case of *Bald/Brunet*, that is expressed in the musician-poet's frequent escapes into the pristine, idealized world of childhood. In *Nijinsky*, it is expressed through the schizophrenic dancer's autonomy of genius, which proves to be a justification even for his insanity. Naturally, the two plays have different textures. Gink created a jazzy mix that blows hot or cool depending upon whether the action is colored most by the irreverent Brunet's bold sarcasm or by the Bald Man's almost painful vulnerability. On the other hand, Burykin's highly poetic play flows on with an elegant grace, not because the characters occasionally speak in verse, but because the dialogue and the situations that create the play's reality seem to hang just beyond the reach of quotidian banalities. But despite their differences, both plays contain that tangible, vital, human warmth that always seems to mark even the most relentlessly probing works of Russian literature.

Other moments linking the plays are more superficial or even technical. Each incorporates poetry (*Nijinsky*) or poetic structures (*Bald/Brunet*) into its text; each often streamlines the dialogue through the use of "questionnaires," i.e., running lists of shotgun questions and answers; and each contains references to the two founding fathers of modern Russian poetry, Alexander Pushkin and Mikhail Lermontov. Although the images and functions of these two giants of Russian literature are quite different in each play, it is significant that their authoritative names, specifically, should crop up at a time of major cultural upheaval and reevaluation. Burykin deepens his link with the literary tradition by repeatedly playing on parallels with Fyodor Dostoevsky's novel, *The Idiot*.

---

[3] Nicolas Berdyaev, *The Russian Revolution* (Ann Arbor: University of Michigan Press, 1971), 2.

Even extra-textual elements unite the writers and their plays. Both are graduates of the Moscow Art Theater School (Burykin from the acting department in 1990, and Gink from the directing department in 1992), and both began writing for the theater almost by accident. Gink wrote *Bald/Brunet* after his friend and classmate Oleg Babitsky said he would like to stage something about two people who "sit around and talk," but that he could not find any plays he liked. It was not long before Babitsky was rehearsing Gink's freshly-written play at the Stanislavsky Theater. Burykin wrote *Nijinsky* at the behest of his friend, the actor Oleg Menshikov. Having just performed the role of Sergei Yesenin in the London production of Martin Sherman's *When She Danced* (for which he received the Laurence Olivier award in 1992) Menshikov was not satisfied with the types of roles he was being offered. As Burykin tells it, Menshikov knew his friend occasionally tried his hand at writing, and he suggested the idea of a play about Nijinsky. The result was the basis for one of the most exciting and most talked-about productions of the 1992–1993 season in Moscow.

For awhile, the subsequent development of the two young writers also followed a similar pattern. Each of their second plays was a talented script for a single-actor play based on the classics. Burykin's *Bashmachkin*, adapted from Nikolai Gogol's story, "The Overcoat," opened to high praise in February 1994, while Gink's *Katerina Ivanovna* is an intense exploration of that seemingly minor, but endlessly fascinating character in Dostoevsky's great novel, *Crime and Punishment*. Staged by Kama Ginkas, one of Moscow's finest directors—and Daniil Gink's father—*Katerina Ivanovna* premiered under the title of *K.I. from "Crime"* at the Young Spectator Theater in November 1994. But even for some time before that, Gink had begun moving away from the theater, becoming involved in the study of his Jewish religious and cultural heritage. Meanwhile, Burykin tired of working on miniatures and threw himself into what he called "a five-act play with tons of characters."

It should come as no surprise, then, that for all the striking similarities that join Gink, Burykin and their plays, *Bald/Brunet* and *Nijinsky* are written in very different keys. Naturally, when brought to life on the stage, they give rise to vastly differing performances.

Bald/Brunet can be a highly deceptive script. When discussing the translation into English, the author himself noted that little in his work is said or done without a healthy dose of self-deprecation. That is visible in the two main characters' smart-aleck rhymes, their lame aphorisms, and in their mock Homeric dialogue in which they pompously act out the parts of the imagined characters of Aquinius and Thermostocles. But the play's heavy irony is most obviously carried in the mercilessly corrosive language and behavior of the character of the Brunet. As the alter ego of the somewhat dreamy, tenaciously idealistic Bald Man, he is ever challenging, irreverent, disrespectful and uncouth. His primary goal is always to cut away the myths and the silly delusions that have crept into the Bald Man's perceptions of himself and his life. Beyond that, the Brunet is also something of a composite, representative of the social forces that act on any individual. He is the one who beats down the Bald Man's defenses, who ridicules his penchant for sentimentality, who drags him, sometimes almost violently, out of his touching, childlike state into a world that is vulgar and cruel. In many ways, *Bald/Brunet* is a play about the struggle of lyricism to survive in surroundings that are hostile to it.

When reading or preparing to produce *Bald/Brunet*, it would be easy enough to focus primarily on the Brunet's scornful, mocking tone. But, in fact, the play is not built on the Brunet's loud, aggressive behavior; it is supported and given its basic form by the essentially quiet, contemplative nature of the Bald Man. It begins with a prologue in which the rarely unified Bald/Brunet team reminisces about random events and objects from his—or their—past. This "listing" of people, places and things—marked by a sad, even wounded intonation—prefigures the emotions and the states that will predominate in the course of the play. The images that arise most often are those of childhood and fear.

This is echoed, although in a very different context, in the finale, which Gink separated from the body of the play and entitled "The Bald Man's Dream." There, for the first time, the Bald Man frees himself of his prickly double and, coincidentally or not, slips back into a childlike state of innocence and purity. There, he regains both the wisdom and the independence which finally allow him to escape the Brunet's constant nagging, although it also leads him to an inevitable end. Perhaps, in fact, it is even the breaking of the dynamic between the two which is the impulse that brings the Bald Man face to face with death. By an attractive coincidence, Gink's allegory of the dying—in which the fearless die as if in a gentle embrace and the fearful die in a terrible frenzy—is quite concisely defined by an entry in Vaslav Nijinsky's diary. "Death," wrote the ailing dancer, "can be lovely when it is God's wish, dreadful when it is without God."[4]

The biggest point of contention between the Bald Man and the Brunet, for all their hifalutin and lowbrow arguments about art and philosophy, is a woman. Perhaps a more symbolic image than a full-blooded character, she is an enigmatic mother-figure at her first appearance, a primarily threatening, sexual image at her second visit, while, in her third appearance, she plays the role of the wise, comforting grandmother who is capable of bridging the gaps between birth and death, childhood and old age. In all cases, the Young Woman is the catalyst that brings out the Bald Man's strongest objections to the Brunet's irascible manner. And it is their behavior in her presence which most clearly illuminates the breach that separates them.

---

[4] *The Diary of Vaslav Nijinsky*, ed. Romola Nijinsky (Berkeley: University of California Press, 1973), 112.

The Brunet frequently accuses the Bald Man of being crazy, and at times the Bald Man himself suspects it is true. That, of course, is a dramatic ruse, a challenge thrown down by the author to force a closer look at the play and at what it says about its central figure. The Bald Man's behavior is "deviant" only in that it differs from the norm of "usual, adult male behavior." He is hurt and thrown off balance by the brutal intrusion of adult life on his childlike dreamworld. During their second meeting, the Young Woman observes that the Bald Man has a "painful, naive harmony" about him, and, indeed, that may be the best and most succinct definition of his character. His journey in the course of the play takes him in search of the lost harmony of childhood. The lists of objects and the strings of aphorisms which recur throughout the play might easily be seen as fragments of the Bald Man's raw, unprocessed memory, a litany of seemingly unconnected experiences which the Bald Man recites not because he suffers from mental illness, but because his mind works with a child's ingenuousness. When discussing strategies for translation, Gink emphasized the importance of the childish lisp in which the Bald Man occasionally speaks, indicating that a child is incapable of having the aggressive, angry emotions that crop up so readily in adults. His purpose was not merely to imitate the sounds of baby talk, but to give the Bald Man a mannerism that would link him directly to the innocence of childhood.

The images of *Bald/Brunet* and the impulses that gave rise to them are all quite concrete. Anyone familiar with life in the Soviet Union (the play was written in the Soviet Union's final year of existence and premiered just weeks before it was officially dissolved) will recognize the "grubby, padded work coats," the "stairwell landings," the "courtyards," the "clackety-clack" of tram cars, and any number of other prominent landmarks of the Soviet Russian landscape. For those who know St. Petersburg (or, more properly, Leningrad) there are several fleeting moments, such as the Bald Man's reminiscences of stone lions, bronze horsemen and "filigreed railings of bridges across the river," which obviously evoke the images of that unique city of which Gink is a native son. But none of these examples of "local color" need stand in the way of a production for a western audience. Appropriately enough, even the Moscow production de-emphasized the specific social and cultural aspects in the play, making of it a powerful, timeless allegory. Gink wrote a highly flexible and theatrical work which raises the particular to the level of the universal.

If, in *Bald/Brunet*, the two main characters often spend their time drubbing one another in fits of anger and frustration, in *Nijinsky*, the title character and his double, the Actor, are locked in the grips of a tense, but dignified, duel. From the play's marvelous opening words of "I'm free! I'm free!" to Nijinsky's spectacular, flying exit, Burykin carefully leads his bifurcated hero through a labyrinthine journey of self-discovery. This is the world of insanity as seen through the opposite end of the looking glass, wherein clinical or social notions of insanity are entirely beside the point. Within the confines of the work, Nijinsky's madness is neither an affliction nor a tragedy; it is a haven that cradles and protects the former dancer's genius. And genius, in Burykin's play, is nothing less than a living spark of God's wisdom and power.

That is certainly one of the reasons why *Nijinsky* is so extraordinarily buoyant. For all the tension arising in the thrusts and parries between the two characters, the play soars lightly from dialogue to dialogue, from scene to scene. Even in its rare dark moments, it is always permeated with the faint perfume of approving, ironic humor. Nijinsky-the-character almost never doubts the divine origin of his nature. That gives him not only the confidence, but the right to tease, to ignore or to scorn that half of his personality which is incapable of grasping the great mystery of genius. It frees him of those mundane responsibilities which bind others to the laws of civilization and the world.

Burykin himself delights in evading the traditional laws of drama. From his determination of the play as "a game of solitaire for two" in the subtitle, to Nijinsky's parting leap at the end, Burykin repeatedly shifts most everything just a hair off center. That is not to claim for *Nijinsky* the status of an experimental or avant-garde work. More properly, it is a play that is based on a poetic structure, in the sense that poetry also uses the language and structures of everyday speech, while skewing and reshaping them to create a denser, more suggestive picture of the things they describe.

Whatever the case, there is no doubting that *Nijinsky* will give a director reason to pause before calling the first rehearsal. How does one incorporate Nijinsky's verse "visions," wherein he is visited briefly by his parents, Sergei Diaghilev, his wife, his daughter and even his unborn son? Who plays them? Nijinsky? The Actor? Do they share the exchanges? Burykin gives no answers in his stage directions. Where does the action take place, and what, in fact, really happens in the course of the play? The author clearly ridicules received notions of plot, using Nijinsky as his mouthpiece. In Act II, the former ballet star says with a tangible air of disgust: "Oh, plot! It's always the same. 'What's the plot of your story?' There is none."

Indeed, in *Nijinsky*, the largest concentration of "useable information" emerges from the atmosphere and the tendencies of the play rather than from the actual reality of it. When Nijinsky is seriously trying for the first time to merge with the Actor in Act II, he explains how he was able to "hang in the air at the top of a leap," and encourages his partner to try it himself. The author provides a brief description of the scene as the Actor finally gathers the nerve to try it:

Nijinsky waves his hand, the Actor starts running. He leaps and flies into the air. Both carefully watch the trajectory of the Actor's leap and laugh at that moment when they imagine he comes back to earth.

Clearly, this is not a routine stage direction merely intended to put the actors in their proper places or have them speak with a prescribed intonation. We only learn that it is an imagined scene after the Actor has "flown through the air" and we, together with the characters, have followed the "trajectory of his leap." In fact, there is no leap. Burykin here is less interested in action than in mood and motivation. More important than the actual event or non-event is the poetic aura in which it is seen, simulated or imagined. (Gink angles for a similar affect in *Bald/Brunet* when he stipulates in Act II that the Brunet *"somehow* finds himself on the top of the closet," or in the finale that the "closet explodes into pieces.")

More categorical, and more difficult to realize from a production point of view, is the stage direction in the finale of Nijinsky which indicates that *Nijinsky* "disappears in a leap." This time, the author provides no attenuating explanations, offering the unusual vision as an unquestioned fact. And, by finding ways to realize this near-violation of physical reality in performance, every production of *Nijinsky* will carry that seed of poetic suggestiveness which Burykin planted everywhere in the play's very structure.

Nijinsky's is a world in which intuition is the greatest moving force. He abhors anything connected to theory or logic, which, for him, smack of categorization, banal definition, or limitation. Even when he deigns to define himself, his definition is so rambling that it hardly defines anything at all. He is, he says, "a bear a bison a dolphin," he is Buddha and Christ, he is "anywhere and everywhere," "love and eternity." Despite constant prompting and cajoling on the part of the Actor, Nijinsky for the longest time refuses to remember his past, his profession or even the Actor's—i.e., his own—name. He simply will not let himself be so cornered.

Of the two characters, Nijinsky is the purer, the higher and the lighter, but the Actor—at least dramatically—is the more complex. If the alter ego bearing the name of Nijinsky essentially represents the divine mystery of genius, the Actor is something of a grab bag into which everything else is tossed. He is Nijinsky's rational half; he is the body into which genius temporarily settled; his attitudes are those of one whom society is usually willing to accept as normal; and—perhaps paradoxically, perhaps not—he ultimately is the one who is most visibly afflicted by something resembling madness. He commences his journey looking and sounding like a one-track-minded psychiatrist whose mission is to draw Nijinsky out of dementia, but things actually progress in the opposite direction. Gradually, the Actor is stripped of his confidence in facts, logic and reason, until, as the play approaches its end, he blurts out in frustration that he somehow got mixed up in "something incredibly absurd." But in a bit of a reverse image of the Bald Man freeing himself from his "double" while reverting to a childlike state, the Actor's admission of his confusion suddenly brings about a temporary peace with his alter ego. Almost immediately, Nijinsky lays claim to his own name for the first time, and the Actor, also for the first time, finds the inspiration to speak in rhyme and even take a stab at a Nijinskian, flying leap.

Nijinsky rings with the clarity and purity of a bell struck sharply. A play about genius, talent and inspiration, it exudes the inspiration and the vision of its author. It offers few explanations, tenders no excuses and everywhere celebrates the exciting, liberating vitality of the divine, creative impulse.

Bald/Brunet and *Nijinsky* offer fascinating glimpses into the tumultuous process that was gripping Russian society as they were being written. But their especial achievement was not just in capturing the textures and peculiarities of social or spiritual upheaval. More important is that, even while eloquently expressing the uncertainty which pervades their individual worlds, they each pinpoint those eternal values which Russian culture has always valued in the past and will certainly continue to value in the future. They are contemplative, philosophical, incisive, and, at moments, even reverent.

But, for all their undeniable Russianness, there is nothing parochial or provincial about these two plays. *Bald/Brunet*, in many ways, is a thrusting effort to get on top of, and come to terms with, the clichés that have divided Russia from the occidental world for the better part of the 20th century. No one will confuse the world portrayed in it with America or even Western Europe, but the author's purview clearly includes an instinctive feel for those cultures. Written only shortly after the fall of the Berlin Wall, *Bald/Brunet* is largely free of the traits that so often made works of Soviet literature appear as strange missives from the dark recesses of an alien, inaccessible land. Gink's aging, disillusioned man from the counter-culture is no longer the old political dissident or even the drunken social outcast. He is what he would probably be were he to show up anywhere else in the world: a bit of a misfit, a spiritual vagabond and a seeker for the truth.

On a more superficial level, *Nijinsky* also shows signs of the rapprochement between the East and the West. Vaslav Nijinsky was a Russian dancer who achieved his legendary status only in Europe. He was categorically opposed to the consequences of the Russian Revolution, which was more than enough to keep his name in a perpetual state of limbo in the former Soviet Union. To be sure, his greatness was recognized, but he was kept curiously distant from the mainstream of Russian culture, which has always embraced its greatest artists heartily. Burykin's play was essentially the first major step taken to find a proper place in the Russian pantheon for the great dancer. What makes it such a significant step is that it wastes no time or effort polemicizing with the hackneyed, distorted images from the past. In fact, Burykin was not the least interested in history, biography or even cultural legacies. He went straight for his hero's most essential, most universal quality: his value as a carrier of spirituality.

INTRODUCTION

Both *Bald/Brunet* and *Nijinsky* were written on clean slates, without prejudice, without malice and without an agenda. That makes them important mirrors of the society—and of the world—that gave rise to them. It is sincerely hoped that these translations, both done in close consultation with the authors, will give English-language directors, actors, audiences and readers an opportunity to gain insight into some of the concerns of the new Russia, as well as an opportunity to see themselves in a new light.[5]

JOHN FREEDMAN
Moscow, 1995

---

[5]I wish to thank Timothy C. Westphalen and Curt Columbus for the valuable suggestions they made after reading drafts of the plays in this volume.

Bald/Brunet

By Daniil Gink

BALD/BRUNET

CHARACTERS

THE BALD MAN — *a balding man, about 50 years old*
THE BRUNET — *a brunet, about 20 years old*
A YOUNG WOMAN — *in her 20s or 30s*

ACT ONE

PROLOGUE

BRUNET. Yellow lamp. Yellow moon. Winding courtyards. Warehouses. Barking dogs. Dogs nipping at your heels.

BALD MAN. The sea. Rocks. A lonely cliff disappears into the sea. I run on it. A man is following me. I try to fly. I fly, but low and slowly. Somebody grabs my legs.

BRUNET. A wooden pier. Rotted clean through. I dive off it. Summer. A sleigh. A horse is pulling it. People are everywhere. Everyone is shouting.

BALD MAN. A coliseum. Covered with a teapot sleeve. I ascend the steps. I eat a chicken leg. It's night. It's cold.

BRUNET. Mountains. Rock. A bear. He's holding an axe. An enormous leaf folds around me. A one-legged sorcerer. He leaps like he's on springs. He sniffs with his long nose.

BALD MAN. An empty house. An empty room. Angular light. I lie on the floor. I'm wearing a furry hat with ear flaps. A plumber comes. He's wearing a grubby, padded work coat. He grabs an ear flap on my fur hat. He drags my hat across the floor.

BRUNET. Train tracks. Grass. Money fluttering in the wind. I stuff some in a tin box. I stuff more in. The box is empty. I stuff more in. The box is empty. I open the box. The box is empty.

BALD MAN. A stairwell landing. Two apartments. Kids hanging out. The water is going to be turned off. I have a baby. I ask the kids for a handout.

BRUNET. I hold out a three-liter jar. The kids toss coins in it. And marbles and jacks.

BALD MAN. The worst thing is, when they turn off the water, you can't just boil water from the pond. First, you've got to let the dirt settle.

BRUNET. The worst thing is, I can't bathe my baby. I have a baby. I don't want to bathe him in pond water.

BALD MAN. My elementary school teacher comes up and says, "You can't bathe babies in pond water."

BRUNET Who's throwing things? Those aren't kids. That's a Gypsy caravan. They're dirty. Their money is filthy.

BALD MAN. I hide from her behind the door. Her nose is falling off. It's turned all black. I bet it's gonorrhea. She might infect my baby.

BRUNET. I hold out a huge, empty jar. I hold it as if it were a baby. I snap a plastic cap on it and begin rocking it.

BALD MAN. My neighbor's door opens. Inside there's a dirty pond with matted grass. The Gypsy caravan makes itself at home and scatters paper all around.

BRUNET. I open my door. I run with my baby to the bathroom. I have to bathe him. I see a yellow lamp in the entryway. I run through the hallways and rooms.

BALD MAN. The Gypsies chase me. They want to take my baby away. I hide in the cupboards and closets. I slip into one of them. I see a street, the night, warehouses, a yellow moon and barking dogs.

BRUNET. I run into one of the warehouses. I crawl up the steps. It's night. It's cold.

BALD MAN. I start rocking and warming my baby. I race through my apartment, looking for the bathroom. I sit in a sleigh. A horse is pulling it very slowly. The Gypsies are gaining on me.

BRUNET. I want to fly. I can barely get off the ground. They grab me by the legs and begin diapering me. Me and my baby.

BALD MAN. They diaper me and sniff me with their long noses. I'm afraid they'll infect my baby.

BRUNET. I'm afraid my baby will suffocate while they're diapering us. We've got to make it quick with the bath. Or they'll take him and bathe him in that filthy pond.

BALD MAN. I start barking. Dogs come running and nip at the Gypsies. I'm too weak to stand up. Too weak to go bathe my baby. The dogs nip at the Gypsies. They shout and ride in a sleigh. But the horse is slow and the dogs are leaping and biting in a frenzy. I feel sorry for the Gypsies. I rock my baby. I lie on the floor, wrapped in a coarse woolen blanket. I'm wearing an overcoat. The blanket is tucked into a sheet. I'm holding a jar with a plastic top. I rock it, and the coins, marbles and jacks in it rattle and jangle. A dog comes up and lies on my head. A yellow lamp shines above me. I'm wearing a fur hat on my head. A room. Angular light. The plumber bangs on the pipes and then comes up to where I'm lying on the floor. He grabs my fur hat by one of the ear flaps and drags it across the floor. He holds an enormous wrench in one hand. In the other, he's holding my hat by one of the ear flaps. He's in a grubby work coat. I'm in an overcoat. I'm holding a jar, lying on my back and I can see his big iron wrench dangling over my glass jar. He walks with a bouncy gait. Like he doesn't even know he's dragging me behind him on the floor.

(A free-standing closet is situated at center stage. From inside it we can hear the piercing sounds of a saxophone. Enter a balding man of about 50 years of age)

BALD MAN. All right, that's it. I've had it. Enough. Cut it. Calm down. Settle down. *(Hammers on the closet with his fists)* Thatta boy. Cool it, now. Cool it. *(Faces the closet, exhales quickly and forcefully as though mustering courage. Opens the door. A saxophone is hanging inside)* One, two, three—chill out, now. *(Takes the sax and tries playing a few notes. Enters the closet and closes the door)*

(We hear a series of low notes interspersed with long, piercing high notes. The young Brunet leaps out of the closet)

BRUNET. *(Wails on the sax)* All right, that's it. I've had it. Enough. Cut it. Calm down. Settle down. Tha-a-a-a-tta boy. *(Exhales quickly and forcefully as though mustering courage)* I don't care if I'm bugging the neighbors upstairs. I don't care if I'm bugging the neighbors downstairs. I don't care if I'm bugging the neighbors next door. I don't care if my neighbors are bugging me from one side or the other, from above or below, from left or right, from up or down or upside down and all around! I don't care if I suffocate in moth balls—God-damned, stinking, sweet, bitter, bittersweet, old-fashioned, retarded, wimpy, dried-out, caked-over, crusted-up, worthless, friggin', floggin', flakin' moth balls. I don't care if I croak and rot.
VOICE OF THE BALD MAN. *(From inside the closet)* You do too, you liar.
BRUNET. No I don't. I don't care. You're the one who cares. Shut up. Sit there and shut up.
BALD MAN. *(Coming out of the closet)* Yeah, well I care. I care a lot.
BRUNET. So is that what you almost busted down the closet for?
BALD MAN. Say what you want, but that's what every problem boils down to.
BRUNET. Except for ones of life and death.
BALD MAN. Problems of life and death aren't for mortal greenhorns.
BRUNET. Or mortal Don Juans. Or mortal neurotics.
BALD MAN. Yeah. Or mortal neurotics.
BRUNET. I don't care.
BALD MAN. So tell me, what do you care about?
BRUNET. Me?
BALD MAN. You.
BRUNET. You.
BALD MAN. Me?
BRUNET. I care about the solidity and longevity of this closet, here.
BALD MAN. You're an idiot. I'm sick and tired of you, you know that? You exhaust me. When are you going to shut your trap, you dweeb? This bald old man wants some peace and quiet. *(He sits down next to the closet. Silence)*

(The Brunet combs the Bald Man's bald head)

Get out of here, will you?

(The Brunet disappears into the closet)

I've got heartburn. My feet ache. My ears are stuffed with cotton. Maybe I'm sick?

BRUNET. *(Sullenly, from inside the closet)* As healthy as a horse. Want me to take your blood pressure?

BALD MAN. Forget it. Maybe I'll have some tea.

BRUNET. *(From inside the closet)* The tea-pot burned up. There aren't any matches. They turned off the gas. The electricity exploded. No tea leaves grew this year. They're rationing sugar.

BALD MAN. Glad to meet you, where's your bathroom?

BRUNET. *(From inside the closet)* Sorry. The weather just isn't cooperating, is it?

BALD MAN. That's all right. That's all right. No problem. I'll just sit here awhile.

BRUNET. *(From inside the closet)* You do that.

BALD MAN. You ought to show some respect for your elders.

BRUNET. *(From inside the closet)* Look who's talking.

BALD MAN. Shut up, you numskull. Give me a break.

(Pause. Quiet rustling and muttering is heard from the closet)

Finally. I'm almost asleep.

BRUNET. *(From inside the closet)* Here.

(A hand holding a plaid blanket reaches out of the closet. The Bald Man takes it and covers himself)

Rough day, huh?

BALD MAN. *(Mutters)* I'm sleeping. I'm sleeping. Just like a baby. I'm sleeping, sleeping, just like a baby.

(The Brunet pokes his head out of the closet)

BRUNET. Say what?

BALD MAN. Shhh.

BRUNET. *(Whispers)* What?

BALD MAN. Shhh. He's sleeping.

BRUNET. Who? Who's sleeping?

BALD MAN. Him. That one.

BRUNET. Where?
BALD MAN. *(Sleepily)* Over there. *(Waves his hand weakly)*

(The Brunet heads in the indicated direction)

(The Brunet alone. Harsh, show-like lighting, harsh, show-like sounds, a show-like costume as if he were a stand-up comic in a comedy club)

BRUNET. Our life. Life is a game. A game of tiddlywinks. Tiddlywinks and canned food. Canned food and barracks. Our life is an outhouse. Outhouses stink. Stink attracts flies. Flies attract disease. Our life is a game in an outhouse. With stinking canned food, flies trapped in jars and pestilent barracks. Our barracks are teeming with pestilent life. A true friend. A friend is a brother. A brother's a bother. A bother's a loser. A true friend is a dog. Dogs have fleas. Fleas come in millions. A true friend is a dog and a brother—a flea-bitten bother and human loser. A true friend is a human loser. A human friend is a true loser.

Those are my latest aphorisms. Oh, yeah. And here's my latest poem. It's called "Shitting, Not Living."

> I've got to quit cussing,
> Fucking and drinking.
> Knock off smoking and washing,
> Shitting and not living.

Here's another one. It's called "From the Summons of the Central Committee of the Communist Party of the Soviet Union to the Residents of the City of Samarkand."

> Our unity, strivings and friendship
> Make our enemies rattle sabres and shields!
> People of Samarkand! Out to the fields!
> Harvest all those old dried potatoes!!!
> Long live the communists! Down with all NATOs!

Do you know the difference between family life and family happiness? Me? What about me? Do you know? Do I know? You. Me? M-e-e-e-e? You. Me. I know. Family life is when you have a wife and family happiness is when she's at work. No! Family life is when you have a wife and a mother in-law. And family happiness is when you're at work, your wife's at a school meeting, your mother-in-law lost the keys to the apartment and her neighbor friend is out buying groceries. Hi there. Hi there. You from the housing committee? No, I'm your wife's nephew from the country.

    If you grew up in the country, you'd better love tractors and dung.

    If you grew up in the city, you gotta sniff smog and read papers.

    If you like philosophy, you're best off not being born.

First I had a tick. Then I got an ulcer. Then I got a mother-in-law and now they're taking me to my grave. If the grim reaper breaks his scythe, all he has to do is grab one of the sickles off one of our hammers. If we didn't have electric ovens, we'd have electric chairs. If we didn't have gas ovens, we'd have gas chambers. And since we have uranium deposits, then that gives us a chance to at least hope that they won't replace our steam heating with atomic space heaters. My advice to foreigners: Count to 73. And at every single number, cut off a beefy piece of your own flesh. Then, maybe, you'll understand what our country went through. My advice to women: If you want to know what it's like to be a sexually frustrated man, plug up every hole in your body and try to sneeze. My advice to children: Don't be like your parents. Otherwise, your kids will be like you. My advice to myself: Think before making wisecracks. And now, my latest poem. It's called "About Life."

> I feel like cussing a blue streak,
> I haven't the foggiest notion why.
> But the reason couldn't possibly be simpler:
> 'Cause life is just like that, that's why.

(The Brunet sleeps under the plaid blanket. For all intents and purposes, the Bald Man is alone)

BALD MAN. Rockabye baby, on the tree top.
          When the wind blows, the cradle will rock.
          When the bough breaks, the cradle will fall.
          Down will come baby, cradle and all.

I love sleeping on my stomach with my hands stuffed under the pillow. I love sleeping when it's raining or snowing outside. Most of all, I love sleeping in a country cabin with a crackling fireplace, or in a train with lights flickering past the window. The lights flicker, the train sways and I always get wherever I'm going. I walk out of the train station, and the town greets me with its emptiness. Especially if it's one that you came to for just a day or two, or if it's the one you grew up in and you've returned to it, knowing in advance that you're going to forsake it and leave it again. In trains, you have to ride in the upper berth. And you have to take cold

8

fried chicken wrapped in aluminum paper. You have to travel light. And you have to see to it that nobody meets you. And when you're at a country cabin, it's got to be wet and damp, and the bed has to be really springy— with two mattresses. And there has to be a morning fog. It should be somebody else's cabin and all the things around you should be old and alien. The smells should be unfamiliar and the blankets should be made out of coarse wool. The fireplace crackles, a snowstorm is whipping and it's deathly silent.

Rockabye baby, on the tree top.

A Christmas tree, decorations and toys made out of cotton wadding are a child's Yuletide dream. Bread, a bottle, sardines and cigarettes are a grownup's Yuletide dream. My Yuletide dream is a bottle, Christmas tree decorations, sardines and somebody else's country cabin. My dream is fried chicken wrapped in aluminum wrap, some soap, a toothbrush and a train. My dream is cigarettes, some dried, pressed flowers, a rough wool blanket and autumn. My dream is a quilt, some pencils, a bottle and winter.

When the wind blows, the cradle will rock.

The morningtime city isn't conducive to people. It's conducive to stone lions and bronze horsemen. Well, then, I'm a stone lion. I'm a gilded griffin. I'm a morning sphinx. The morningtime city isn't conducive to people. It's conducive to the clackety-clack of a tram car, the rat-a-tat-tat of ice clattering down a drain pipe, the wham! wham! slamming of doors. Then, I am a drain pipe. Then, I am a tin roof. Then, I am the filigreed railing of a bridge across the river. The city in the morning is conducive to the damp scent of the river, the damp scent of wooden girders, the damp scent of bricks, the damp scent of smoke rising from a burning pile of wet leaves, the astringent scent of oil on the tram tracks. Then, I am the scent of leaves. Then, I am the scent of smoke. Then, I am the scent of mist.

When the bough breaks, the cradle will fall.

I love sleeping on my stomach with my hands stuffed under the pillow. Daytime, nighttime, morning, evening. Only, there shouldn't be anybody around. There should be nothing but dead, empty silence. There should be nothing but autumn or winter. In the autumn I dream transparent dreams. In the winter I dream eternal dreams. Autumn dreams are a water drop, winter dreams are the rattle of ice. Autumn dreams are a lovely sound, winter dreams are a droning hum. When autumn dreams become winter dreams—that's what I call a miracle.

Down will come baby, cradle and all.

A-a-a-a!

BRUNET. *(Steps up)* Nah, nah, rockabye baby. Listening to you makes me sick.

BALD MAN. Yeah?

BRUNET. Sick to my stomach. You make me wanna puke.

BALD MAN. Listen. I... you... uh...

BRUNET. What? Well, what? You look like a kindergarten rug-rat who crapped his pants. Only I'm not your nursemaid. God, I hate it when you start sniffling and whimpering! Wah-wah-wah. *(He disappears behind the closet)*

(We hear the sound of running water and somebody washing up. The Bald Man sits absentmindedly. The Brunet enters in a tee-shirt, shrugging his shoulders. His face has red blotches on it from having washed in cold water. A damp towel is tossed over his shoulder and he's holding an electric teapot)

Here. *(Gives the Bald Man the towel and goes to plug in the teapot)*

(The Bald Man goes behind the closet to wash up. The Brunet mutters like a baby—wah-wah-wah!—and moves around the table and chairs. He puts teacups and breakfast on the table and starts cutting up some salami. The Bald Man, shrugging his shoulders just like the Brunet, comes out from behind the closet in a tee-shirt. He sits down and watches the Brunet with a blank expression on his face. The Brunet pours some tea, sits down and starts wolfing down his breakfast)

(With his mouth full) Go on, eat. I feel like I tied one on.
BALD MAN. I'm eating. *(He eats)* Flick it on.
BRUNET. Huh?
BALD MAN. Flick on the radio.
BRUNET. *(With his mouth full)* What a bore.
BALD MAN. Huh?
BRUNET. I said, the radio is a roaring bore.

(The Bald Man turns on the radio. They both eat silently and listen to a silly, old-fashioned children's program)

This is really stupid.
BALD MAN. It reminds me of my happy childhood. Especially in summer camp.
BRUNET. There he goes whimpering again!
BALD MAN. God dammit, this is my home you know! I'll say what I damn well please.
BRUNET. You say what you damn well please at work. And at home you turn into a whimpering baby. It's downright pornographic.
BALD MAN. You're a retard.
BRUNET. A what?
BALD MAN. A retard, an inhibited, spiritual retard.
BRUNET. *(Howling with laughter)* Finally! That's the stuff! That's more like it. We ought to write that one down. Go on, write it down.
BALD MAN. You write it down.

BRUNET. I will, I will. *(Goes to the closet, writes on the side wall)*

BALD MAN. Yeah, that's not bad. You could do a show out of that: The Spiritual Retard.

BRUNET. And his sidekick, the sexual muffball.

BALD MAN. That's me, I suppose.

BRUNET. Nah, you're a sexual pinhead.

BALD MAN. Thanks.

BRUNET. Any time. Bon appetit. Happy listening. The main thing is to avoid constipation.

BALD MAN. Carry on, carry on, my little moron.

BRUNET. What I carry is a hot stick of salami in my mouth.

> I grabbed my thing and made it hard.
> Hey, hey baby, wanna drive my car?

BALD MAN. The anthem of a virgin.

BRUNET. I love you for your wit
>> And all your hifalutin shit.
>> But every time you spill your guts,
>> You know, you only drive me nuts.

BALD MAN. With your brain like a poison snake,
>> Go on, walk tall, big dude.
>> You may be young and wimpy,
>> But you got a knack for being rude.
>> But, go try it in the streets,
>> They'll kick your face, big kid.
>> And maybe then you'll see
>> The sufferings of this ol' bald head.
>> And if you still don't get the point, son,
>> Watch you don't get slipped some poison.

BRUNET. Period. Morning's a bad time to be writing rhymes.

BALD MAN. I agree. What were you doing crawling in the closet yesterday?

BRUNET. A simple case of despair.

BALD MAN. Looking for your socks in pairs?

BRUNET. I thought we were through with that.

BALD MAN. O.K., O.K., O.K.

BRUNET. All right. So, what do you have to offer besides a closet?

BALD MAN. Why don't you go down to a museum and take in some great art?

BRUNET. Jesus! How come it is you always make me want to put out a cigarette on your teeth?

BALD MAN. Take in a ballet. Go to the theater.

BRUNET. Too many people.
BALD MAN. I don't know, I don't know. Well, do something, for godsakes. Conceive a kid. Plant a tree. Write a book.

(Pause)

BRUNET. A little baby boy is born. O, happiness! O, diapers! O, baby crib!
BALD MAN. Baby powder, diapers.
BRUNET. Then comes kindergarten.
BALD MAN. Nah, I'll educate him myself.
BRUNET. What about your job? Where you gonna get the time?
BALD MAN. So what's a wife for?
BRUNET. Can you imagine yourself with a wife?
BALD MAN. No.
BRUNET. Me neither.
BALD MAN. Then it looks like we can forget the kid.
BRUNET. What were the other possibilities?
BALD MAN. Plant a tree.
BRUNET. Earth, seed, rain. A little sprig. It grows into a thick trunk. Then comes autumn and then comes winter. And then your little tree withers.
BALD MAN. What if it doesn't?
BRUNET. Then some jerk'll cut it down.
BALD MAN. Well, it looks like it's "write a book."
BRUNET. Oh no. That's your specialty.
BALD MAN. No thanks.
BRUNET. In that case, plant a tree, cut it down, saw it up, make a coffin and use it.
BALD MAN. You mean there's no other alternative?
BRUNET. You're a dead man.
BALD MAN. Now, wait a minute. Let's go back to the first choice. A woman.

(The Brunet laughs)

What's so funny, pinhead?
BRUNET. I remember that wondrous moment[1]
      When you appeared before me,

---

[1]This poem by Alexander Pushkin may be the most famous in the Russian language. Hardly a Russian does not know it, and there certainly is no Russian who has not had it shoved down his or her throat in school. It is infinitely more beautiful than can be shown by any translation. The playwright suggests that a director of an English-language production might replace Pushkin's poem with an equally well-known poem from his or her own national tradition.

BALD MAN. Imbecile.
BRUNET. Like an ephemeral vision,
BALD MAN. Knock it off.
BRUNET. Like a spirit of pure beauty.
BALD MAN. Shut up!
BRUNET. In the languors of hopeless sorrow,
       And the anxiety of the daily race,
       I hearkened your voice so tender,
BALD MAN. Shut — Up!
BRUNET. And dreamed of your beautiful face.

(The Bald Man hammers on the closet with his fists. The door swings open and he slams it shut. The Brunet keeps reciting the poem and the closet door keeps swinging open. The Bald Man angrily keeps shutting it. The Brunet triumphantly recites the poem, the Bald Man angrily slams the closet door)

> The years passed. Dreams
> Were scattered by violent gales.
> I forgot your voice so tender,
> The heavenly features of your face.
>
> In grim, obscure confinement,
> The days were long and slow:
> No faith, no inspiration,
> No tears, no life, no love.
>
> Then again my soul awakened:
> And you again appeared to me
> Like an ephemeral vision,
> Like a spirit of pure beauty.
>
> My heart now beats in rapture,
> Again it is teased and moved
> By faith and by inspiration,
> By tears, by life…[2]

BALD MAN. Get outta here!
BRUNET. What a bore! *(He disappears into the closet and closes the door behind him)*

(The Bald Man begins cleaning things up. He washes the dishes, sweeps up crumbs, hangs his jacket in the closet, waters the flowers. The doorbell rings. The Bald Man opens the door and returns with the Young Woman)

---

[2]The Brunet is interrupted before reciting the final words: "by love."

YOUNG WOMAN. Excuse me, but may I sit down? Maybe you could bring me a glass of water.
BALD MAN. Aren't you feeling well? Wait a second, I'll be right back. *(Leaves)*

(The Young Woman sits and smiles enigmatically. The Bald Man returns with a glass of water)

Here you are. *(Gives her the glass)*
YOUNG WOMAN. Thank you. *(Drinks)*
BALD MAN. What's wrong? Should I call a doctor?
YOUNG WOMAN. No, no. That's not necessary. I'll just sit here a bit. It'll pass. *(She smiles)*
BALD MAN. Maybe you'd like some more water?
YOUNG WOMAN. No, I feel better now.
BALD MAN. Perhaps you're hungry?
YOUNG WOMAN. No, it wasn't from hunger. *(She smiles)*
BALD MAN. What do you keep smiling for?
YOUNG WOMAN. I doubt you would understand. You're a man.
BALD MAN. Ah, so it's something strictly female, is it? Oh, I'm sorry. That was a tactless question.
YOUNG WOMAN. Don't worry about it. You really haven't guessed, have you?
BALD MAN. No. What was I supposed to guess?
YOUNG WOMAN. You remind me of my father. Don't you notice anything? *(She smiles)*
BALD MAN. You were a little bit dizzy and sick to your stomach.
YOUNG WOMAN. Are you married?
BALD MAN. No.
YOUNG WOMAN. *(Laughs)* Then you won't be able to understand.
BALD MAN. Why?
YOUNG WOMAN. I haven't interrupted anything, have I? If you were doing something, go right ahead with it. I'll just sit here awhile.
BALD MAN. Please do. You just sit right there. It's been a long time since I had guests.
YOUNG WOMAN. I can see that you are lonely.
BALD MAN. You can?
YOUNG WOMAN. Of course.
BALD MAN. Strange. *(Pause)* You are a brave woman. All by yourself, you just walk right into a strange man's apartment.

(The Young Woman stares intently at the Bald Man)

YOUNG WOMAN. On the other hand, you are extremely trusting.

BALD MAN. I think maybe I ought to be afraid of you.

(The Young Woman smiles. Pause)

  I get the feeling that you're someplace else.
YOUNG WOMAN. Oh? Where am I?
BALD MAN. Someplace else.

(Pause)

  What?! What's wrong? Are you feeling ill again?
YOUNG WOMAN. Calm down, calm down. Everything's all right. *(She smiles)*
BALD MAN. Are you talking to me?
YOUNG WOMAN. Of course not. I'm talking to it.
BALD MAN. To what?
YOUNG WOMAN. Shh, calm down. Sleep, sleep, little one.
BALD MAN. Who are you talking to? There's nobody here.
YOUNG WOMAN. Yes there is.
BALD MAN. Where?

(The Young Woman smiles)

YOUNG WOMAN. There you go. Sleep, sleep. That's my little sweetie. You're going to be smart. And wise. And beautiful. Your mama loves you. And your mama is waiting for you. Don't be afraid. Mama will be there to help you. There you go.
BALD MAN. Oh, I didn't get it at first. *(Smiles)*
YOUNG WOMAN. But now you do?
BALD MAN. Yes.
YOUNG WOMAN. It's sleeping again. Goodbye now. *(She leaves)*
VOICE OF BRUNET. *(From inside the closet)* Sorry. I got carried away.
BALD MAN. Ah, forget it. I did, too. I'm the one who's sorry.
VOICE OF BRUNET. Man, we live a drab life.
BALD MAN. Yeah. Thanks for keeping quiet while she was here.
VOICE OF BRUNET. No problem, my man. I understand.
BALD MAN. You and I fight a lot.
VOICE OF BRUNET. It's just the generation gap.
BALD MAN. Generation gap? What the hell are you talking about?
VOICE OF BRUNET. There you go again. *(He comes out of the closet)* Wanna sit for awhile?
BALD MAN. Sure. *(He goes into the closet and shuts the door)*
BRUNET. You wouldn't be able to live with her, anyway.
VOICE OF BALD MAN. *(From inside the closet)* Why not?

BRUNET. You're too egotistical!

VOICE OF BALD MAN. How do you figure?

BRUNET The closer someone is to you, the more demands you make on them.

VOICE OF BALD MAN. You think so?

BRUNET. Yeah. I consider that natural for an artist.

VOICE OF BALD MAN. And?

BRUNET. That's all. I don't want to put it in words. Otherwise the whole thing falls apart.

VOICE OF BALD MAN. I'll invite her to come visit me.

BRUNET. What for?

VOICE OF BALD MAN. We'll drink tea and talk.

BRUNET. What if she comes with her husband?

VOICE OF BALD MAN. What husband?

BRUNET. You don't think she's a single parent, do you?

VOICE OF BALD MAN. I didn't think about it.

BRUNET. He's probably one of those idiots who comes home and reads the newspaper in his slippers.

VOICE OF BALD MAN. What do you think she'd have a husband like that for?

BRUNET. What the hell difference does it make what kind of husband she has? A husband is "a thing unto itself." Once you've got one, you've got one forever.

BALD MAN. *(Flinging open the closet door)* That's it! Forget it! She's an idiot!

BRUNET. There you go!

BALD MAN. And you're a jerk! You ruined everything! What the hell did you have to go bring up her husband for? Idiot!

BRUNET. Oh, shut up. We'll see yet which one of us is the idiot. *(Goes into the closet and slams the door shut)*

(Pause. The Bald Man knocks quietly on the door)

(From inside the closet) Leave me alone!

BALD MAN. I'm sorry.

BRUNET. *(From inside the closet)* Get outta here!

BALD MAN. All right! *(He goes into the closet and closes the door)*

VOICES. *(From inside the closet)* Get out of here! Get out of here yourself! I was here first! I don't give a damn! I don't give a damn if you don't give a damn! The hell with you! The hell with you, too! Quit drooling on me when you shout! You think that was me drooling on you!? What do you think this is, then!? Pigeon droppings! What pigeon!? The one you let out your ass! Look who's talking! Speak for yourself! Keep your hands off me! Then quit shoving! I'm not shoving anybody! And I'm not talking to you! Me either! Ape! Parrot! You're a fat, hairy ape! You're a fat, hairy parrot!

(A long silence, followed by hysterical laughter)

What's your problem? I started thinking about a fat, hairy parrot.

(The second voice begins laughing hysterically)

O.K., I'm getting out. It's stuffy in here.

(The Bald Man comes out of the closet)

BALD MAN. But you're an ass, if I ever saw one.
BRUNET. *(Coming out of the closet)* What did you say?
BALD MAN. I said, "hee-haw!" You ass.
BRUNET. Which one of us is the ass if it's you going around hee-hawing? You're sick.
BALD MAN. Who's sick? I'm sick?
BRUNET. Write it down, nurse: "Beastomania." Plus paranoia and brain damage. Put him in an isolation cell.
BALD MAN. You're the one who's sick!
BRUNET. Hello! How are we today? How's your schizophrenia doing? Is it behaving itself like a submissive wife? Doing the shopping, washing the clothes and fixing lousy dinners? I see. Hey nurse, get this man a divorce and we'll fix him up like new. And who are you?! Yeah, you. Who are you?! Oh, I see. Run-of-the-mill epilepsy. Hey, nurse, get me a pot, quick. I can feel an involuntary urge to urinate coming on. Hello, are you next? Put everything out here, now. Nice and easy. Take that key out of your mouth. Take my glasses out of your nose. Give the nurse back her wig. I can't help it nurse, I'm a kleptomaniac. Next! Wait a minute. There's another one here. *(To the Bald Man)* How are you, today, patient?
BALD MAN. What the hell is your problem?
BRUNET. Are you in a psycho ward or not?
BALD MAN. I'm at home.
BRUNET. And I say you're in a psycho ward.
BALD MAN. You're the one in a psycho ward.
BRUNET. Patient! Don't talk back to me like that! I'm old enough to be your father. Otherwise, it's off to the isolation cell with you. With no mail privileges.
BALD MAN. All right, all right. What do you want from me?
BRUNET. Nothing at all. The point is, what do you want from me, patient? What's your problem?
BALD MAN. Nothing.

BRUNET. Nothing? Let's have a look at your record.

BALD MAN. What's wrong with me?

BRUNET. It says here you're suffering from l-l-l-o-g-o-r-r-r-h-e-a.

BALD MAN. What the hell is that?

BRUNET. Th-th-th-th-at's wh-wh-wh-en y-y-y-ou c-c-c-on-stantly re-p-p-p-eat ev-v-v-erything.

BALD MAN. Yeah? Very interesting. Good. Th-th-th-ank you, d-d-d-octor.

BRUNET. *(Also stuttering)* Wh-wh-wh-at's wrong, p-p-p-atient? You af-f-f-raid of s-s-s-omething?

BALD MAN. N-n-n-o.

BRUNET. Wh-what is it, th-th-en?

BALD MAN. I've g-g-g-ot the h-h-h-i-ccups.

BRUNET. Th-th-at's not the h-h-h-iccups. You're st-t-t-uttering.

BALD MAN. Y-y-eah? W-w-ell that's wh-wh-why I'm saying "h-h-h-iccups" and not "st-t-t-uttering."

BRUNET. O.K. We'll say you're h-h-h-i-ccupping and not st-t-t-uttering. It happens to lots of people. Don't be af-f-f-raid.

BALD MAN. *(Stops stuttering)* O.K., doctor. I won't. Only tell me honestly, what do I do if sometimes I feel like putting on a noose instead of a tie?

BRUNET. *(In amazement)* So that's it? However, what's the difference? *(Stops stuttering. Begins speaking rapidly and writing down the answers to his questions)* Do you urinate?

BALD MAN. Yes.

BRUNET. Blue?

BALD MAN. Yellow.

BRUNET. Hot?

BALD MAN. Yes.

BRUNET. Good! Appetite?

BALD MAN. No.

BRUNET. None?

BALD MAN. Yes.

BRUNET. For long?

BALD MAN. Yes.

BRUNET. Good! Women?

BALD MAN. What?

BRUNET. Women, yes?

BALD MAN. Yes. What women?

BRUNET. Yes, what? Women, yes?

BALD MAN. What women yes?

BRUNET. Yes, women yes, or yes, women no?

BALD MAN. Yes, women yes. What do you mean, no? No, women yes.

BRUNET. Yes or no?!

BALD MAN. No.

BRUNET. So is it yes or no?!

BALD MAN. Yes!
BRUNET. Men?
BALD MAN. No.
BRUNET. Men, yes?
BALD MAN. No!
BRUNET. Good! Give me a number!
BALD MAN. Five.
BRUNET. Color?
BALD MAN. Black.
BRUNET. Scent?
BALD MAN. Smooth.
BRUNET. Taste?
BALD MAN. Sour.
BRUNET. Lenin?
BALD MAN. Bald.
BRUNET. Stars?
BALD MAN. Red.
BRUNET House?
BALD MAN. White.
BRUNET. Smoke?
BALD MAN. Pipes.
BRUNET. Fights?
BALD MAN. Home.
BRUNET. Knock?
BALD MAN. Door.
BRUNET. Teeth?
BALD MAN. Dentist.
BRUNET. Butter?
BALD MAN. Cheese.
BRUNET. Bread?
BALD MAN. Crumbs.
BRUNET. Fleas?
BALD MAN. Roaches.
BRUNET. Window?
BALD MAN. Rain.
BRUNET. Rain?
BALD MAN. Cops.
BRUNET. Cops?
BALD MAN. Rain.
BRUNET. Rain?
BALD MAN. Cops.
BRUNET. Cops?!
BALD MAN. Rain.
BRUNET. Rain?

BALD MAN. Cops.
BRUNET. Cops!!!
BALD MAN. Caps.
BRUNET. Caps?!!
BALD MAN. Cops.
BRUNET. Cops?
BALD MAN. Caps.
BRUNET. Cups?
BALD MAN. Cops.
BRUNET. Cups!!!
BALD MAN. Cops.
BRUNET. Vodka?
BALD MAN. Disgusting.
BRUNET. Yes.
BALD MAN. No.
BRUNET. No?
BALD MAN. Yes.
BRUNET. Full steam ahead, hurrah!
BALD MAN. Slogans.
BRUNET. Slogans? That's interesting.
BALD MAN. Red.
BRUNET. Red?
BALD MAN. Stars.
BRUNET. Stars. Of course. Stars?
BALD MAN. Torso.
BRUNET. Torso? Very interesting.
BALD MAN. Naked.
BRUNET. Aha! Naked?
BALD MAN. Woman.
BRUNET. Woman?
BALD MAN. Grandpa.
BRUNET. Grandpa?
BALD MAN. Prince.
BRUNET. Prince?
BALD MAN. Bedtime story.
BRUNET. Bedtime story?
BALD MAN. Bird.
BRUNET. Bird?
BALD MAN. Flip.
BRUNET. Flip?
BALD MAN. Coin.
BRUNET. Coin?
BALD MAN. Taxi.
BRUNET. Taxi?

BALD MAN. Home.
BRUNET. Home?
BALD MAN. Closet.
BRUNET. Closet?
BALD MAN. Loneliness.
BRUNET. Loneliness?
BALD MAN. Rain.
BRUNET. Rain?
BALD MAN. Cops.
BRUNET. *GOOD!*
BALD MAN. S-s-o, wh-wh-at's m-m-y p-p-problem, d-d-doctor?
BRUNET. A cut and dried case, p-p-p-atient. You've got to deep-six that cop
  who's trailing you, or, better yet, emigrate somewhere.
BALD MAN. Hell no. I don't even want to hear about it. What the hell
  would I do there?
BRUNET. Where? In prison after you get convicted of murder?
BALD MAN. No, in some foreign country. Those aren't joking words, you
  know.
BRUNET. Well, if we're not joking, then let me ask you a serious question.
  What's wrong with emigration?
BALD MAN. It's not so bad here… *(Scratches his neck)*
BRUNET. I don't need you to tell me what's good and what's bad here.
  What I want to know is why you think that things here are better than they
  are worse?
BALD MAN. What makes you think I think things here are better than they
  are worse?
BRUNET. Because you're a numskull. A manure bug. A dissident. A half-
  wit with masochistic tendencies. Where in the hell else would someone
  like you live? And then, of course, as they say, your roots are here.
BALD MAN. That's right. They are. Right here. Right here. Right here. I
  never knew that before. If I wound up in one of those fat, self-satisfied,
  over-fed countries, do you think a local girl would come up to me and say
  I remind her of her father? I can picture it now. The doorbell rings. I open
  the door and—what do you know—there's some sleek creature in a
  designer gown standing there.
  "Hello," I say.
  "Hi there," she says. "How are you?"
  "Fine," I say.
  "Hey baby," she says, "I was at one of your concerts."
  "Is that so, tootsie?"
  "Pour me a glass of whiskey," she says, "I've gotta talk to you."
  "I've got nothing but vodka, baby," I say.
  "Oh, yeah," she says, "they told me you were Russian. Well then, pour
  me a glass of the stinking juice. Only make mine with soda water."

"Have a seat," I tell her, "and drink up. You've got a great pair of legs."

"Thanks," she says, "I know. Hey, you know what, baby? You remind me of my old man."

"You don't say? How's that?"

"He was gay and he used to look at women just like you do."

"You think I'm gay? There aren't any gays in Russia."

"Don't lie to me, hotstuff. There was this one Russian guy I wanted to sleep with, but he stole my boyfriend before I could get him into bed. But I can tell you're not gay."

"You've got nothing but gays hanging around you, sweetheart."

"Yeah, that's what happens to kids whose daddies spent their whole life kissing their boss's ass."

"What can I say, baby? Sorry to hear it."

"The worst part is that he dumped me and my old lady when I was seven. So I ended up hanging out with druggies."

"You poor baby."

"Yeah, and then the whole narco squad started taking an interest in me."

And on and on and on. And then she asks me to become her father— says she wants me to give her fatherly caresses. But I refuse. So she threatens to sue me and write a letter to *Time Magazine*. I give in and start caressing her. Then, before you know it, I drag her into bed. I drag her into bed and we spend the whole night tripping the light fantastic. When I wake up, she's in the bathtub. And when she comes out, she says, "Hi, baby."

"Mornin', tootsie."

"You're really hot, baby. Thanks."

"It was nothing, tootsie. Here's some money for a cab."

"Hey, baby, knock it off," she says. "I can drive myself home in my Lincoln."

"So, you're a millionaire, are you?"

"Nah, it's my old man who's the millionaire. The Lincoln was a birthday present."

"Gave it to you for your seventh birthday, did he?"

"No. Last year. I was just lying about all the rest. See ya."

"See ya later, sweetheart."

And after that I spend a couple of months in detox trying to recover from the trip.

BRUNET. Bravo! That's a great story. You ought to write it down.

BALD MAN. *(Suddenly exploding)* I'm never going to write down nothing anymore! I am telling you that if I'm going to live in shit, I want it to be my own! I can't live anywhere but here! The shit I need's right here and I can't live without it! If I wrote all that down and read it to those morons, they'd never understand jack. They'd just laugh at me, the pathetic jerks. Stinking swine!

(The Brunet goes into the closet from which we can hear Louis Armstrong singing "Sometimes I Feel Like a Motherless Child." The Bald Man calms down slowly)

I'm going for a walk. *(Puts on his coat)* Autumn is here.

(Autumn leaves fall from above and the wind blows them around the stage. The Bald Man walks among them)

Hello, hello, hello. I'd like to begin with a poem called "Dissident Lyricism":

> If shit didn't stink
> And tasted like sugar,
> No one would dare compare
> Shit and the U.S.S.R.

(Opens up a notebook and writes lazily)

Very good. What's so good about it, sir? What's good, my good sir, is that we still haven't lost the ability to distinguish between the taste of shit and the taste of everything else. *(Writes in his notebook)* Say, have you been through some terrible ordeal? Yeah, I was just reading my passport. It says right there in black and white: "Citizen of the Union of Soviet Socialist Republics." And following that is my name. *(Writes in his notebook)*

> A brick climbed up the wall
> And another followed it there.
> Who cares where bricks will crawl?
> Maybe their nest is up there.

(Writes in his notebook)

What do you do if your wife is a lesbian? Sleep with her AC/DC.

(Writes in his notebook)

What does a soldier kiss?—The flag.
What does a student kiss?—The teacher's hand.
What does a General Secretary kiss?—His mother-in-law.
What if he's not married?—Then he kisses his own ass for having sat through so many congresses and meetings.
What does a minister need a chair for?—So he'll have something to stand up from when his boss enters the office.

Can a communist be impotent?—Yes, if his wife stops singing revolutionary songs to him at bedtime.

A man listened to the radio and decided to go deaf. A man watched the television and decided to go blind. A man ate in a cafeteria and decided to go hungry. A man went out on the street and decided never to go anywhere again. A man offered his hand to his neighbor and, when he found out his neighbor was a Stalinist, he cut off both hands. A man thought about all these things and went out of his mind.

What's left to bury when he dies?—One great big ass.

Do you want to die?—I want to die politically unaligned.

How do you envision the future?—As a flourishing garden.

You mean here in our country?—No, throughout the whole world.

What will our country be like?—A manure pile to fertilize the world's garden.

Do you agree with the proverb: "Reap as ye shall sow"?—Yes. We sowed socialism and communism and now we are reaping famine and military dictatorship.

Love, equality and brotherhood was the slogan on the French revolutionary guillotine. Peace, labor, May was the slogan on many Soviet buildings.

What color is a Soviet citizen most afraid of?—None, because he's color-blind. He peers into the future and sees nothing there but emptiness.

Would you want to be Lenin?—No, because after I die I don't want them to stuff me with sawdust so that endless hordes of people can walk past me and think to themselves, "You son-of-a-bitch."

Tell me, what time is it?—Past curfew.

This is me, this is my wife, and this is an x-ray of my dog's left leg.

A policeman stopped a diplomat's car and asked for his license. So the diplomat said, "I have license to do what I damn well please."

Hello, I'm calling about your ad. Are you the one who wants to exchange an apartment with a ghost in it?—Yeah, only you should know that he's a drunkard and isn't legally registered to live here.

How much does a Soviet condom cost?—A ruble a pack and fifty rubles for the abortion.

> I love big-breasted women
> There can be no doubt about it.
> When I come home battered and broken
> I like sleeping on a soft, loving tit.

(The Bald Man sits down next to the closet, leans against it and falls asleep.)

BRUNET. A small operating table for newborns. He lies on it naked and diapered. Two grown women examine him, counting his fingers, poking his belly-button and birthmark. They move his legs, peek in his ears and squeeze the backs of his knees and the folds of his arms. They ooh and aah with silly little smiles and then they pull out a syringe and give him shots. The needles sink into him as if he were boiled meat—there's a small jerk, but it's painless. As though it were someone else's body. Then, there he is lying on the same table, his long legs cocked up over his buttocks and his shoulder blades hanging over the edge. He's naked again and his bald head looks just like a baby's. His body is all tensed up because the table is too small to hold him. The more he strains, the redder his face gets. He thinks his belly-button is going to unravel, but, instead, a small lizard crawls out absolutely painlessly and runs across his bald head before falling on the tile floor with a damp, slapping thud. His skin is white and his broad-boned body is covered in birthmarks. His body is tense and he is freezing cold in the rays of light from the operating lamp. Two very young, but probably very silly, women lean over him, blowing coldly and lightly on those parts of the male anatomy which are most prone to excitement. The girls are dressed in crinoline and Turkish hats. His immature male parts lay helplessly in a flaccid heap. The Turkish hats fall on the tile floor and roll around on it. The women laugh and blow.

Obviously, this is a dream. Please, turn out the lights.

END OF ACT I

ACT TWO

(The closet is at center stage. Sounds of the saxophone are heard from inside. The Bald Man appears. He is frail and appears to be ill. He leans heavily against the closet. The saxophone continues to play for a moment and then there is silence. The saxophone plays again, and then there is silence. A knock comes from inside the closet. The Bald Man lifts his head and there is another knock. The Bald Man drops his head again. There is a sudden, loud bang on the inner wall of the closet. Pause. The Brunet pokes his head out of the closet)

BRUNET. What's wrong?

(The Bald Man is silent)

What? You mean those bums finally got to you?

(The Bald Man is silent)

Forget the bums. Grab your sax.

(The Bald Man is silent)

All right. *(He comes out of the closet and tests the temperature on the Bald Man's forehead)* Everything O.K. there. *(Opens the Bald Man's mouth and peers down his throat)* Everything O.K. there. *(Tests the mobility of the Bald Man's knees)* Healthy as a horse. What he needs is a woman. You want a woman?

(The Bald Man is silent)

Listen, maybe you've lost your potency?

(Pause)

BALD MAN. Maybe.

(The Brunet whistles gaily as he sits in the open closet)

    Who needs it?
BRUNET. There's a question for you.
BALD MAN. More to the point is, what do I have to offer?
BRUNET. Now, that almost sounds like a joke: What do I care about impotency, and what does impotency care about me? Sounds to me like the first line of a poem.
BALD MAN. You want to write a poem?

BRUNET. Go ahead. It's better than lying around like a used condom.

(The Bald Man is silent)

Want some tea?
BALD MAN. I'll fix it.
BRUNET. Yeah, you got it bad.
BALD MAN. No, I'll fix it later.
BRUNET. *(Speaking to the closet)* I'll just sit here mum and quiet. I'll pretend I'm not here. Just like he's all alone here in this room and he's talking to himself. As if, maybe, he's gone off his rocker or is just a wee, wee bit insane. Maybe if he's all alone, he'll own up to what happened. *(He sits and whistles as if he doesn't notice anybody)*

(A short pause)

BALD MAN. Maybe I'm in the wrong line of work.
BRUNET. *(Whispers loudly to the closet)* Here we go! Now we'll find out what's wrong.
BALD MAN. And maybe sometimes I don't behave so good.
BRUNET. *(To the closet)* Pay no attention. He's talking to himself.
BALD MAN. A little bit too uncouth.
BRUNET. *(To the closet)* Well, that's something we'd already noticed, now, isn't it?
BALD MAN. Maybe I oughta clean up my act.
BRUNET. *(To the closet)* Listen to this guy go.
BALD MAN. Kick it all to hell.
BRUNET. *(To the closet)* I don't know about you, but I can't take this anymore. *(He plugs up his ears)*

(The Bald Man is silent. The Brunet sits, plugging up his ears. Pause. The Brunet unplugs his ears and talks to the closet)

Did he say anything? No? *(He's amazed)* In that case, he's working up to the stupidest thing he could possibly say. *(He plugs up his ears again)*
BALD MAN. I'm exhausted. And I'm getting too old. Who needs it, anyway? I mean, maybe I should start up a family? Ha. There's a good idea.
BRUNET. *(Unplugging his ears, speaks to the closet)* What did he say? Yeah? Are you kidding? I don't believe it! O.K. I got you. Thanks. *(To the Bald Man)* Are you nuts? Did you lose your marbles? Are you wacko? I'm telling you, you're an inflamed abscess on the body of the Soviet family.
BALD MAN. Maybe I should take up music again.
BRUNET. What? What did you say?!

BALD MAN. You know, hook up with some little band as second sax.

BRUNET. *(With interest)* And then what?

BALD MAN. Or maybe not. Maybe I'll go solo. I'll call my act, "A Saxy Monologue."

BRUNET. Go on, go on, go on.

BALD MAN. For a long time I've been wanting to…

BRUNET. For a long time you've been wanting to write with sounds instead of words.

BALD MAN. *(Happily)* Yeah.

BRUNET. Yeah, that would break down the barriers and give you the emotions you're looking for.

BALD MAN. Yeah!

BRUNET. Yeah, and then you could skip around all those inner contradictions.

BALD MAN. *(Jumps up and starts pacing)* Yeah!

BRUNET. Yeah! And what you'd get is milk-toast music, pabulum pop.

BALD MAN. Yeah! I've been wanting to go public with my secret closet-music for a long time!

BRUNET. Yeah! But who gives a damn what you play in your lousy closet?

BALD MAN. *(Suddenly cooling off. Grimly)* Nah. That saxophone already almost killed me once. To hell with it.

BRUNET. Say what? Say what? What sweet memories have we remembered this time?

BALD MAN. *(Louder)* To hell with it.

BRUNET. It's all for the best.

BALD MAN. *(Muttering under his breath)* To hell with it all.

BRUNET. *(To the closet)* Still, the old neurotic got wound up there for a minute. Just like a little kid.

BALD MAN. It's all for the best.

BRUNET. Yeah, you're probably right. Anyway, I already said that. But then, all your jokes are ass-backwards.

BALD MAN. If only thirty years ago…

BRUNET. Twenty-six years ago.

BALD MAN. If only they hadn't told me I didn't have any coordination…

BRUNET. And if only they didn't tell you that you got no musical ear, no sense of rhythm and you can't improvise your way out of a paper bag—in other words, if they hadn't told you that you were a no-talent—then you would have been a great musician. Bullshit. You just got lucky, man. Everybody was doing it and you just did it a little bit better. That's all. Even if everything they told you was a pack of lies.

BALD MAN. I'd still be doing what I'm doing now.

BRUNET. *(To the closet)* Looky there. This man's nobody's fool.

(The closet door opens on its own with a creak)

28

See there? Even you agree with me.

BALD MAN. Shut your trap, you heap of trash. (*Kicks the door closed*)

BRUNET. Hey dude, what are you doing kicking around your best friend?

BALD MAN. If I ever get around to starting a new life, the first thing I'm doing is selling this closet.

BRUNET. First they betray their friends, and then they betray their country.

BALD MAN. Do you remember when was the last time I had guests?

BRUNET. Yeah, it was when you told a whole crowd they were impotent. Artistically speaking, that is.

BALD MAN. I think we were discussing whether theater, in particular, is a waste of time, and art, in general, is a sin.

BRUNET. Yeah, you said that art reminds you of some greasy bum who gets ahold of a killer broad, undresses her and then doesn't have the foggiest notion of what to do with her.

BALD MAN. I still say art is nothing more than vanity.

BRUNET. Uhuh, and you said that artists don't do anything but beg the public to kiss their ass.

BALD MAN. I don't understand how somebody can say, "I can't help but write," "I can't help but compose music," "I can't help but produce plays." People are born to expiate their sins and struggle against temptation. Everything else is self-indulgence and hypocrisy.

BRUNET. You called 'em all a bunch of hucksters.

BALD MAN. You know, it occurs to me: Maybe art is one of the great temptations?

BRUNET. Something tells me you're getting serious on me. Let's try a new tack. (*Disappears behind the closet and then reappears looking like a Roman philosopher*) Tell me, Aquinius, memento mori? Or perhaps, after all, vita brevis, ars longa?

BALD MAN. (*As if suddenly coming to his senses*) What did you say, pinhead?

BRUNET. Hurrah! I would engage thee in a philosophical dialogue about the eternal problems. Thou shalt be Aquinius. I shall be Thermostocles. Wouldst thou don thy laurel wreath?

BALD MAN. You know, I'm in the mood for a good talk.

BRUNET.
  Didst thou hear, Aquinius mine, whose wisdom is all-embracing,
  That, only yesterday, as the sun settled into the omnipotent sea,
  I created an aphorism of blinding wit and revery?

BALD MAN.
  I did. For, as thou gazed upon the sea that gently kissed the sandy shore,
  I heard thou sayst with all the splendor of a bold, swift box upon the ear:
  "If boundless reason gives form to each and every possibility,
  And if the body, au contraire, is trapped in eternal captivity,
  That means my paltry body and its blood that flows within are but a lie.

That means mine intellect is that great flood of pow'r that lets me fly."

BRUNET.
  Bright Eos then emerged out of the clouds and lightly bent her step
  Toward that place where ancestor Cronus had spread for her a bed.

BALD MAN.
  And in thy madness, thou continued: "Eos is body and Cronus is reason.
  Eos gave us pleasure, but one day she, together with her rosy fingers,
  May set beyond the sea and never rise again.
  And meanwhile, Cronus, that tireless, unseen one,
  Rules over all that can be thought or can be done."

BRUNET.
  What does this mean, Aquinius, who is so filled with wisdom?

BALD MAN.
  Mine answer, Thermostocles, shall be a simple aphorism.
  Cronus is a eunuch, mark thee well, indifferent to all.
  He deals out equal lots to everyone, big or small.

BRUNET.
  Aquinius, friend of candor! How right thou art!
  Though Cronus is barren, his reason bears fruit.
  But answer me this, thou, whose wisdom knows no end:
  How can my body be wracked with the hunger for truth,
  If flesh be but a forgery of reason?

BALD MAN.
  O, pitiable son of Bacchus, heed what I say to thee:
  Flesh is life.
  But Life is there where flesh is not yet born
  And there where flesh has died already.

BRUNET.
  O, wise man! Thou hast led this sheep from darkness.
  Shouldst thou order it, I shall serve thee,
  And shall anoint thy feet with unction.
  For with thine unction thou hast soothed my heart.
  Thou hast filled my imbecilic brain with honey-laden harmony.

BALD MAN.
  Praise me not, Thermostocles.
  Cast not so easily the pearls of thy words,

Lest they be fouled in filth and dirt.

Enough. I'm pooped. I'm making some tea. (*Removes his laurel wreath*)
BRUNET. No! Don't do it! Don't fade away into eternity with your teapot!

'Twould be best to imbibe some young wine...

BALD MAN. Yeah, you would like to poison me, wouldn't you?
BRUNET. Well, have it your way.

(*The Bald Man puts the teapot on the stove and spreads a tablecloth on the table*)

Hey, the fancy one! What is it, a holiday?
BALD MAN. Almost, yeah. You could say it's a holiday.
BRUNET. What's the occasion?
BALD MAN. On this very date of this very year, I finally came to the conclusion that I am sick and tired of everything.
BRUNET. Sick and tired of what? Living? Then what you need is a bar of soap and a noose.
BALD MAN. Most of all, I'm sick and tired of you.
BRUNET. Fathead.
BALD MAN. Speak for yourself.
BRUNET. All right, all right. What did I do?
BALD MAN. What didn't you do? But specifically, who knows?
BRUNET. Oh, no you don't. I want you to be specific.
BALD MAN. Specifically, I don't know. (*Sets the table with tea service for two, cookies and jam*)
BRUNET. Well, you've intrigued me now. However, I don't feel like tea.
BALD MAN. I didn't offer you any.
BRUNET. So we're having guests are we? Or, more specifically, a guest. Seeing as how you burned all your bridges with your old friends, I presume it's a new guest. Pass the jam. Wait a minute, it's not that broad that stopped in here for a glass of water, is it?
BALD MAN. None of your damn business.
BRUNET. So you finally gathered up the nerve. (*Gesticulates*) THAT'S MY MAN! Only you'd better put on a clean set of sheets. It's been a month since you changed the bed.
BALD MAN. Cram it.
BRUNET. Say, did you fix dinner yourself? (*Gesticulates*) Or is she bringin' with?
BALD MAN. Stuff it, jerk.
BRUNET. All right. Let's return to the previous topic. You came to the conclusion that you're sick and tired of everything. What new conclusions can you draw from that?

BALD MAN. First of all, I want people to quit looking at me as if I were a mangy dog.

BRUNET. Since when did you start worrying about what other people think? That's a very interesting turn of events.

BALD MAN. I refuse to continue this conversation. (*Looks around to see that everything is in order on the table and that the room is tidied up. Stares heavily at the Brunet, who stares back at him. The Bald Man tosses a teaspoon on the table and plops down in a chair*) Forget it. It's no good. (*Slinks into the closet and closes both doors behind him*)

BRUNET. (*After a pause*) Little kids always have it tough. But it's a hell of a lot worse for big, bald little kids. (*Somehow, he finds himself sitting on top of the closet*)

"How many times have I told you, son: Don't eat in your school uniform."—"Mama! Weave me awone. I'm thinking."

"What do your parents do at work, sonny?"—"Smoke cigawettes."

"Mama, don't sing! Papa, cut it out!"

"Gwamma, once upon a time Jesus wived on ewth."—"Eat your oatmeal, son."—"Wait a minute, gwamma! Once upon a time Jesus wived on ewth and he was a vewy kind doctow."—"I'm listening. Eat."—"O.K., gwamma. Jesus, he heawed evwybody."—"Yes, he did, sweetheart."—"And then along came a weaw bad Piwate."—"Pirates are very bad, sweetheart."—"Not piwates, gwamma! Piwate."—"Pirate, honey. Pirate."—"I don't want my oatmeal, gwamma. Take it away! Piwate was weaw bad. And he asked evwybody, should we cwusify him ow wet him wiv? And evwybody said, cwusify him. And then they naiwed him up with naiws. And when he asked fow something to dwink, they gave him vinegaw. And then he fwew away to heaven to be with his papa."

When his parents come home from work, they shout: "Grandma! Who's been reading him the Bible?!"

"How old are you, sonny?"—"Shut up, wady. You have cwooked teeth."

"Mama, do we have enough money to buy this toy?"

"Mama, what does p - r - i - c - k mean?"—"That's a man's dinkle, son."

"I'm not talking to you anymowe. I'm gonna go dwaw on the miwwow."

"Weave me awone, ow ewse I'w go cut aww the buttons off youw coat!"

"Stand back, evwybody! I'm gonna jump off the cwoset on the bed."

"Gwanpa, could I sit in youw cwoset?"

Thank you vewy much, evwybody. I'm gonna go bye-bye, now.

(*The doorbell rings. the Brunet jumps down off the closet and quickly disappears inside it. The Bald Man comes out of the closet, suddenly stops, turns around and heads back to the closet*)

BALD MAN. O.K. O.K. That's enough. That's it. All right. Calm down. Calm down, now. That's right. Calm down. That's the way. Easy does it.

(Closes the closet doors) One, two, three: Here we go. *(Goes to answer the doorbell. Silence. He returns with the Young Woman)* Let's not say anything at all. Let's just sit silently and drink tea.

(They both sit down and drink tea)

BRUNET'S VOICE. *(From the closet)* Gertrude, do not drink! The spindle is dipped in poison!

(The Bald Man chokes on his tea and begs the Young Woman's pardon. Teatime continues. The Young Woman serves herself some jam)

If I'm not mistaken, I think it was in that jam jar that we found a bloated cockroach.

(The Bald Man chokes)

BALD MAN. Excuse me. Something seems to have fallen in the closet. *(Goes up to the closet and slightly opens the door. He spits through the crack)*
BRUNET'S VOICE. *(From the closet)* How many times have I told you: Don't spit in the well.
BALD MAN. *(Returning to the table)* I guess I was mistaken.
BRUNET'S VOICE. *(From the closet)* Hey baby, are you sitting there with your legs spread under the table?
BALD MAN. Nope. I definitely heard something fall in the closet. *(Goes back to the closet and whispers)* Shut your goddam trap!
BRUNET'S VOICE. *(From the closet)* Well then, tell her to close up her legs. This is embarrassing, you know.
BALD MAN. *(Whispers)* Shut up!
YOUNG WOMAN. What did you say?
BALD MAN. Oh, nothing. My sport coat just fell off the hanger.
YOUNG WOMAN. Oh.
BALD MAN. Don't pay me any mind. I've lived alone so long that every once in awhile I start acting a little strange. There: Did you hear that?
YOUNG WOMAN. No. Did you?
BALD MAN. Yes.
YOUNG WOMAN. What?
BALD MAN. *(In confusion)* A voice. A voice, of course.
YOUNG WOMAN. What did it say?
BALD MAN. I couldn't possibly repeat it.
YOUNG WOMAN. Come on, you're the one that started it. What did it say?

(Pause. The Bald Man starts laughing)

BRUNET'S VOICE. *(From the closet)* What are you howling about, scumbag?

BALD MAN. It was just a joke! Get it? I was just teasing you!

YOUNG WOMAN. *(Laughs nervously along with the Bald Man)* Oh, now I get it. You were teasing me.

BALD MAN. You're the one who said I'm strange. I'm just trying to live up to your expectations.

YOUNG WOMAN. Yes. You are rather unpredictable.

BRUNET'S VOICE. *(From the closet)* Wait 'til you see what he's like in bed.

(The Bald Man spins around and gives the closet a hard kick)

YOUNG WOMAN. What are you doing?

BRUNET'S VOICE. *(From the closet)* He's a strange-o. A psycho. You've got to keep your distance from his kind.

BALD MAN. What am I doing? I'm just trying to prove that I'm unpredictable.

YOUNG WOMAN. I don't need any proof. I can see that on my own.

(The Bald Man returns to the table and sits down)

BALD MAN. Listen… What I wanted to say was that your last visit caused enormous changes in me.

YOUNG WOMAN. I think…

(In the closet, the Brunet bursts out laughing)

I think you're imagining things. You don't…

BALD MAN. Just one second, please. *(Flies over to the closet and flings open the doors. It is empty)* There. I'll feel better that way. Sorry.

YOUNG WOMAN. You don't have to apologize. *(Smiles)* I got the feeling that I frightened you when I mentioned my father.

BALD MAN. You know, you are a very sensitive person. After you left, I couldn't formulate what had happened to me. But that's not because I thought you are really my daughter. I've never had a wife or a daughter. I was never married. I mean, I lived with women from time to time—a couple of times for several years. But I have a terrible disposition. It was especially bad when I was young. I don't deny it.

YOUNG WOMAN. *(Smiles)* Yes, a bad disposition doesn't facilitate a smooth family life. But I can see you're an excellent friend. I'm sure of it.

BALD MAN. You know, I always thought so too!

YOUNG WOMAN. *(Smiles)* I'll tell you a secret. Sometimes I behave terribly with people, too. And afterwards, I'm always ashamed. Sometimes I'll just be sitting there and, out of the blue, I'll remember something so embarrassing I want to cry.

BALD MAN. I can't imagine what you must look like crying.

YOUNG WOMAN. If you and I become good friends, maybe I'll feel comfortable enough to let down and have a good cry.

BALD MAN. I used to cry a lot at night when I was young. But that stopped when I turned twenty-eight or so.

YOUNG WOMAN. Seeing as how you and I are so much alike, I guess I have another seven years to go on my weepy period.

BALD MAN. You're that young?! Oh, I'm sorry. That was tactless of me.

YOUNG WOMAN. (Laughing) Don't worry about it. I try to look older on purpose.

BALD MAN. Yeah, I would have said you're about twenty-five.

YOUNG WOMAN. Thank you.

BRUNET'S VOICE. (From the closet) Thatta boy. You honed in like a champ on the age hint.

BALD MAN. I'm very happy that you were at my concert. But don't you think that I'm rather crude, spiteful and profane?

YOUNG WOMAN. Yes. But that's just what makes you unique and charming.

BALD MAN. My spitefulness torments me much more than my crudity and profanity. Spitefulness is unbecoming of an artist.

YOUNG WOMAN. I agree with you. That's why I don't like Lermontov very much. But you have a kind of painful, naive harmony about you.

BALD MAN. Pain, yeah. And how nicely you said that—"naive harmony." You know, I've been working on my childhood memoirs. If I ever get around to publishing them, I'll call them "Naive Harmony."

YOUNG WOMAN. (Smiles) That's a risky undertaking. I wouldn't want you to read them to me. I think things like that should remain personal secrets. It would be a shame to publish them. It would be better if someone found them in a dusty trunk after you die. Or even better yet: Burn them.

BALD MAN. How easily you talk about my death. Although I don't deny that I've already tipped past the half-way mark. I don't expect to live to a hundred.

YOUNG WOMAN. I find it very easy to talk about death. (Smiles) The only thing I am sure of in my life is that I'll die. Are you afraid of death?

BALD MAN. You know, I made up an aphorism just like that! There is only one law which has no exceptions: Every person is physically mortal.

BRUNET. (From inside the closet) What is all this about death? Ask her about her husband.

BALD MAN. When I was young I used to think about death all the time. But I was never afraid. My faith in God is unshakeable.

YOUNG WOMAN. Strange, but you are constantly talking about your youth as if you are trying to narrow the age gap between us.

BRUNET. (From inside the closet) I wonder what her husband is up to right about now? Probably soaking his feet or washing his underwear.

BALD MAN. Let's talk about death some more. You have a wonderful way of giving it an inner illumination.

YOUNG WOMAN. You mean, you perceive death as darkness? What good is your unshakeable faith in God, then?

BRUNET. *(From inside the closet)* She's sitting here while he's at home scrubbing his boxers. You've got the perfect chance to score. Only you'll have to adopt the kid.

BALD MAN. Ha! And I thought you didn't pick up on what I said.

YOUNG WOMAN. Not at all. Only it didn't sound sincere the way you said it. I couldn't resist catching you up on it. I warned you that sometimes I behave terribly. But, we were talking about death...

BRUNET. *(From inside the closet)* Talking about hitting up on strangers' wives, I'd say it's about as easy as a heavyweight decking a flyweight. The only difference is there's no blood.

BALD MAN. Talking about death, I have to admit there was a time when I had nightmares about waking up in a coffin. Like Gogol. I was terrified of suffocating. The most horrible thing was that I couldn't lift the top off the coffin because it was covered with six feet of dirt. I have a vivid vision of the blackness and claustrophobia that will seize me at that instant when I open my eyes in my coffin...

BRUNET. *(From inside the closet)* Go on, go on. You've hit on a very interesting thought.

YOUNG WOMAN. All that means is that you're afraid of physical suffering.

BALD MAN. I am amazed at the exquisite simplicity of your thoughts and the ease with which you understand everything.

(The Brunet appears in the closet. He closes the doors)

YOUNG WOMAN. What a strange closet you have. The doors close all by themselves.

BALD MAN. It's my ghost.

YOUNG WOMAN. Joking again?

BALD MAN. Would you like some more tea?

YOUNG WOMAN. No, thank you.

BALD MAN. What were we talking about?

YOUNG WOMAN. Death.

BALD MAN. Basically, if you look at it abstractly, it's a rather disconcerting topic. Maybe we could find a topic more suitable for an evening chat between a man and a woman?

(The Young Woman laughs, gets up and walks around the closet)

YOUNG WOMAN. *(Laughing)* What do you suggest? Surely not love?

BRUNET. *(From inside the closet)* Yeah.
BALD MAN. No. Anything but that.
YOUNG WOMAN. What then?
BALD MAN. I know what! Sit down. I'll read you some of the stuff I've written only for myself. I've never shown it to anybody.
YOUNG WOMAN. You don't think you'll regret it?
BALD MAN. *(Falling into thought)* Maybe I will. But sit down anyway.
YOUNG WOMAN. Are you sure?
BALD MAN. I'm sure. No more questions. Sit down.
YOUNG WOMAN. I'm sitting.

(The Bald Man goes into the closet and pulls several sheets of paper out of the far corner. Closes the doors)

BALD MAN. I won't read everything, of course. Just a few excerpts. A lot is really obscene. And you and I don't really know each other that well yet. Still, I can read some of it to you. *(Bursts into laughter)* No, I'd better not read that one. Here, I'll read something from my cycle, "Thoughts of a Bald Man, Having Seen His Reflection in a Black Marble Column."

> My bald spot in black marble
> Shines like a copper coin.
> While all that reflects in my bald spot
> Looks wonderfully fine!

BRUNET. *(From inside the closet)* What I want to know is what things look like reflected on your ass.

(The Bald Man angrily spins his head towards the closet, then pretends nothing has happened. He continues)

BALD MAN. What is the point of life?—In understanding that it's pointless.
BRUNET. *(From inside the closet)* So what's the point of your idiocy?
BALD MAN. Who doesn't need eternity?—He who knows what it means.
BRUNET. *(From inside the closet)* And who doesn't need me? Tee-hee, tee-hee, tee-hee.
BALD MAN. Can the means justify the ends?—My answer is a question: Is anybody capable of seeing anything through to the end?
BRUNET. *(From inside the closet)* What I want to know is, afterwards, will you ever be able to justify yourself to yourself?
BALD MAN. There are three laws of dialectics: The unity and struggle of opposites; the transformation of quantity into quality; and the negation of negation. And I came up with three more: The struggle of quantity with

opposites; the transformation of quality into negation, and into the unity of negations. But I suppose those are the laws of degeneration.

BRUNET. *(From inside the closet)* If I'm not mistaken, you're getting ready to score.

BALD MAN. I can't read what I wrote here. Oh, yeah. *(Speaks quickly)*

"Do you work in a morgue?"—"No, I just got back from the theater."

"Did you take your kid to the circus today?"—"No, we were at the mausoleum."

"Did you eat something sour?"—"No, I was thinking about my mother-in-law."

BRUNET. *(From inside the closet)* I hope you didn't forget to buy condoms.

(The Bald Man spins around quickly and flings open the closet doors. The Brunet stands there smirking. A short pause. The Bald Man turns to the Young Woman)

BALD MAN. Sorry. I'll feel better that way.

BRUNET. He'll feel better that way, see? And don't you dare try closing these doors, sweetie.

BALD MAN. "Some people kill time, some people kill people. Some people talk trash, some people talk sense. Don't you just want to lay down and die, sometimes?"

BRUNET. Yeah. But I'd rather have some ice cream.

BALD MAN. "Who believes in man? Our Lord God. He's the only one who cares about man."

BRUNET. Who said so?

BALD MAN. Shut up. I'm sorry. "What is self-esteem?"—"Camouflaged self-love."

BRUNET. So when are you going to jump her bones?

BALD MAN. Shut up! I'm sorry. I wasn't talking to you. "What is pride?"—"The result of attributing to yourself qualities you don't have." "What is arrogance?"—"The result of attributing to yourself every quality you can possibly think of."

BRUNET. I'd say it's more like the result of an erection.

(The Bald Man turns toward the Brunet)

BALD MAN. That is silly and disgusting. *(Turns around again)* "Do you eat bread and butter or butter with your bread?"—"Yes, I do eat on occasion."

BRUNET. You eat shit.

BALD MAN. *(Spins around furiously)* Speak for yourself! *(Turns around again)* My God, I'm sorry. "Socialism is possible in a specific given state. But is it possible in a huge, specific mass grave?"

BRUNET. I think he's working up to socialism in a huge, specific bed.

BALD MAN. *(Losing his temper)* I'm going to strangle you! Sorry about that. I'll cave in your face! Excuse me, I'm not talking to you. Shut up, you wimp! Excuse me! "If you go sticking your nose in other people's business, you'd better know their business too."

BRUNET. And if you stick your nose in her…

BALD MAN. Shut up!!! I'm sorry! Get outta here! I'm not talking to you! You animal! You son of a bitch! You worm! Sit down. Please sit down. You whore! Sit down! *(He chases the Brunet in circles around the table so that several of his remarks are addressed in the direction of the Young Woman)* Scum! Trash! Sit down! Come here, you snake! Sit down, I said! I'm not talking to you, I'm talking to him! Come back here, you freak! Beast!

YOUNG WOMAN. *(Speaks while the Bald Man continues to shout)* Shhh. Shhh. Calm down. Calm down. Go to sleep, now. There's nothing to fear. Everything's all right. Now, now, now. Calm down and go to sleep. You just had a little fright. There's nothing to be afraid of. Shhh. Shhh. Don't kick mommy, now. Don't kick mommy. That hurts, sweetie. Calm down, my little love. Everything will be all right.

BALD MAN. I'll kill you!!!

(The Young Woman jumps up and leaves. The Bald Man freezes while he's deciding whether to run after her or keep chasing the Brunet. Finally, he collapses in a chair. Pause)

What's going on? Have I really gone out of my mind?

(Falls fast asleep as if after an epileptic attack. The Brunet approaches him and caresses his head. He covers him with a blanket, goes into the closet and closes the doors behind him)

THE BALD MAN'S DREAM

(The sounds of early morning. Autumn leaves are falling)

BALD MAN. *(Speaking in a childish lisp from here on out)*

> Think of death!
> How does it feel?
> I'm my own man,
> Say what you will.
>
> My hour has come?
> Well, then I'll die!
> We'll shoot the breeze,
> Sweet death and I.

All your life long
You walk with death.
You'll never cheat
Its last short breath.

Death is grace.
Greet it with taste.

BRUNET. Hey son, what are you doing here?

BALD MAN. *(Continues to lisp)* Sitting.

BRUNET. You ought to go home. It's late.

BALD MAN. I'm making poems. What are you doing, mister?

BRUNET. Ha! I'm making poems, too, kid.

BALD MAN. Two people can't make poems in the same place. They get in each other's way.

BRUNET. Well, run on home, then. Where do you live? I'll walk you home.

BALD MAN. I was here first. I always make poems here.

BRUNET. How old are you, boy?

BALD MAN. Six. *(Holds up six fingers)*

BRUNET. Have you been making poems a long time?

BALD MAN. That's my professional secret.

BRUNET. *(Laughs)* Well, it's still time for you to get home. Your parents will be worried.

BALD MAN. Isn't anybody worried about you at home?

BRUNET. No.

BALD MAN. Do you have a wife?

BRUNET. No.

BALD MAN. Me neither.

BRUNET. But you have parents and they're probably very worried about you.

BALD MAN. You have parents, too. Everybody has parents.

BRUNET. But I don't live in the same apartment with my parents. I'm already grown up. I can do that, see?

BALD MAN. Every person is grown up only insofar as his view of the world allows.

BRUNET. *(Amazed)* Where did you read that, boy?

BALD MAN. I don't know how to read yet.

BRUNET. But you can write?

BALD MAN. I don't know how to write yet. I'm still little.

BRUNET. How do you write poems, then?

BALD MAN. You mean you write your poems down? What for?

BRUNET. Well, I don't know. So I don't forget them.

BALD MAN. Whenever I hear pretty, long words, I always memorize them right away.

BRUNET. You can hear your own poems?

BALD MAN. Yeah. But they aren't only mine.

BRUNET. Why? What do you mean? Whose are they, then? Wait a minute, what's that you said?

BALD MAN. It's simple. I have a little friend who isn't born yet. And while he's getting ready to get born, he lives in my head. We talk together all the time. He tells me about everything, because he is older than me. Sometimes I ask him to recite me poems and he does. But, since him and me are almost just alike, they're my poems, too. Because when I grow up, I'm going to think up poems, too. Sometimes he shows me movies. One time I saw a man lying in bed. His face was real pale and dark. He kept chewing ice and there was a whole bunch of people outside the window. There was so many of them that a few people almost got knocked off the pier into the river. Then the man died and everybody cried a lot.

BRUNET. Say, have you ever had a doctor look at you?

BALD MAN. No, but a nurse examined me once when I had a stomach-ache.

BRUNET. And you never went to see her again?

BALD MAN. No. I like talking to you, only you're kinda stupid. You don't understand anything. You ask about one thing and then you start talking about another. I think you have spiders in your head.

BRUNET. What do I have in my head?

BALD MAN. Spiders. Every idea is like a spider. It grabs things and eats them. You know, explains them. Or sometimes it traps everything in webs. I have lots of spider webs in my head and there's a spider sitting on every one. But I think your spiders are blind. They're afraid of everything and they run real fast but they can't catch anything. All they do is bump into each other.

BRUNET. So that's it! Thank you.

BALD MAN. Well, go on, now. You're bothering me. But you can come back tomorrow. Only not for long. Wasted time is an awful crime.

(Amazed, the Brunet leaves. Autumn leaves keep falling. The closet looks like a small hill. The Bald Man sleeps. The Young Woman appears. She approaches the Bald Man, sits down next to him and caresses his head)

Who are you?

YOUNG WOMAN. I'm your great-great-grandmother.

BALD MAN. You mean the one with the music box?

YOUNG WOMAN. That's right. Here, look. *(Opens the music box; it begins to play)*

BALD MAN. Mama has one just like that in our closet.

YOUNG WOMAN. That's right. It's mine. I'm your mama's great-grandmother.

BALD MAN. Great-great-gramma, is it true that when you die you go live in this music box?

YOUNG WOMAN. It's true. That's where I live.

BALD MAN. You mean you already died?

YOUNG WOMAN. Yes. I was born a long, long time ago.

BALD MAN. Does that mean if I was born just a little while ago, I won't die for a long, long time?

YOUNG WOMAN. Yes.

BALD MAN. Where am I going to live when I die? With you in the music box?

YOUNG WOMAN. (Smiles) No, sweetheart. I live in the music box with your great-grandmother and your grandmother. And when your mother dies, she will live with us, too. You'll live in the closet with your great-great-grandfather, your great-grandfather, your grandfather and your father, when he dies.

BALD MAN. But since the music box is always in the closet, that means we'll all live together. I love you great-great-gramma.

YOUNG WOMAN. I love you, too, sweetheart.

BALD MAN. Great-great-gramma, how come your music box plays music but my closet doesn't?

YOUNG WOMAN. I don't know. But your closet smells so sweet of perfumes and soaps.

BALD MAN. Yeah, I like it a lot. I love the way my closet smells. But who lives in the sewing machine?

YOUNG WOMAN. Nobody lives in the sewing machine. It's cold there.

BALD MAN. What about the clock?

YOUNG WOMAN. That's where uncle Death lives. When he comes to see you, don't be afraid. Just ask him what you're supposed to do. He'll tell you everything and show you how to live in the closet.

BALD MAN. I thought death was a woman.

YOUNG WOMAN. Auntie Death only visits bad, guilty people who are afraid of death. Uncle Death comes to those who die peacefully. Uncle Death lives in the clock, but Auntie Death is terribly restless and she flies around in the cold skies.

BALD MAN. Why is Auntie Death restless?

YOUNG WOMAN. Well, I'll tell you, but it's long past your bedtime. Listen carefully, now. A long time ago, Auntie Death and Uncle Death lived together.

BALD MAN. In the clock?

YOUNG WOMAN. No, there didn't used to be clocks. Go to sleep now, or I won't tell you the story. There now. Everyone lived together like brother and sister and nobody ever died because they had each other and didn't need anybody else. But many people liked Auntie Death because she was very pretty. One day, a man who had taken a liking to Auntie Death snuck up on Uncle Death and poked out his eyes. Then Auntie Death went to her father and asked: "How can I take revenge on that man?" And her father said: "Embrace him and kiss him, but no one besides your beloved blind brother should hear you do it." Well, that's what she did and the man fell on the ground and never moved again. But Uncle Death was blind, and he could only hear the kiss. So he went to his father and asked: "How can I take revenge on that man?" But his father said: "You have already been avenged." "No, I haven't," said Uncle Death. "All right," said his father, "then go take his brother by the hand, even though he is guilty of nothing." And Uncle Death went and took the man's brother by the hand. Then the brother fell on the ground and never moved again. But that was Auntie Death's very first embrace and kiss and she became intoxicated by it. So she embraced and kissed the next man she came upon and he fell on the ground and never moved again. But she didn't like that kiss. Suddenly she saw a man who was looking at her in fear because every time she embraced and kissed someone, they fell on the ground and never moved again. She flew after the frightened man and when she caught up with him, she kissed him and embraced him. This kiss was even sweeter than the first, and when she saw him fall on the ground, never to move again, she suddenly understood that the sweetest kisses come from fear and guilt. Just then Uncle Death, who had heard both kisses, came up to her. He recognized his beloved sister by the rustle of her hair. He knew she was deceiving him. And, not realizing what she was doing, she started to kiss and embrace him, too. But he grabbed her by the hand and stopped her. Suddenly she flew into a terrible frenzy and was consumed by the desire for more kisses. But by now, many were afraid of her because she had become horrible. She was insatiable and began swooping restlessly through the heavens, planting kisses on every fearful and guilty man she found. Gradually, she even stopped noticing those who weren't afraid. Uncle Death sat down and listened to the earth creak on its axis. He knew it was a steady, eternal sound. That is when he built the first clock and went to live there to escape the terrible cries of all the frightened people. The din of their voices drowned out the measured ticking of the earth as it turned on its axis. He sat for a long time, contemplating the sound it made. Then his father came to him and said: "There are people without guilt who do not fear your sister. I am not angry at them, and I love them as I love you and your sister. But the lives of all creatures should be as equal and even as the rhythmic sounds of the turning earth. Now, when you think it is time, go to these people and take them gently by the hand so that none should live eternally. Their death may be determined by the pains they have suffered or by the good they have done. But no one ever must twice hear the sounds of the spinning earth."

(The Bald Man sleeps)

(*A free-standing closet is situated at center stage. It is covered in autumn leaves. From inside a melody can be heard. The closet doors open on their own and we see the Brunet and the Bald Man sitting face to face. Both are playing saxophones. It is early morning and a janitor can be heard sweeping in the courtyard. We cannot see him, but we see leaves being swept to left and right behind the closet. Unseen, he slowly moves upstage. The Bald Man and the Brunet play a long, sparring duet, although each seems to be in his own world. The music, which should continue for a long time, is neither gay nor boisterous. The Bald Man finally stops playing. The Brunet continues on, but there is no longer any sound coming from his saxophone. The Bald Man comes out of the closet and puts his saxophone in its case. The Brunet continues to play silently. The Bald Man puts his saxophone case in the closet and removes a music box from there. He puts on his coat and hat and leaves, banging the door quietly behind him. The Brunet continues to play silently as the doors of the closet close slowly on their own. From inside the closet we hear the long, screeching cry of a saxophone. A silent pause. Suddenly, the closet explodes into pieces*)

VOICE OF BRUNET. Abuduh, abuduh, abuduh, that's friggin' all, folks!

CURTAIN
END OF PLAY

1. Pyotr Mamonov, as the Bald Man, and Denis Burgazliev, as the Brunet, in *Bald/Brunet* at the Stanislavsky Theater, Moscow, 1991. (Photo: Mikhail Guterman)

2. Pyotr Mamonov and Denis Burgazliev performing in *Bald/Brunet* at the Stanislavsky Theater, Moscow, 1991. (Photo: Mikhail Guterman)

3. Lyudmila Lushina, as the Young Woman, and Pyotr Mamonov, as the Bald Man, in *Bald/Brunet* at the Stanislavsky Theater, Moscow, 1991. (Photo: Mikhail Guterman)

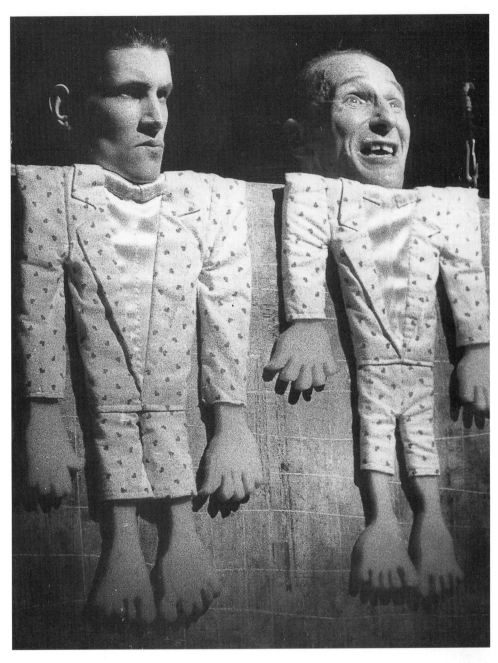

4. Denis Burgazliev and Pyotr Mamonov in *Bald/Brunet* at the Stanislavsky Theater, 1991. (Photo: Mikhail Guterman)

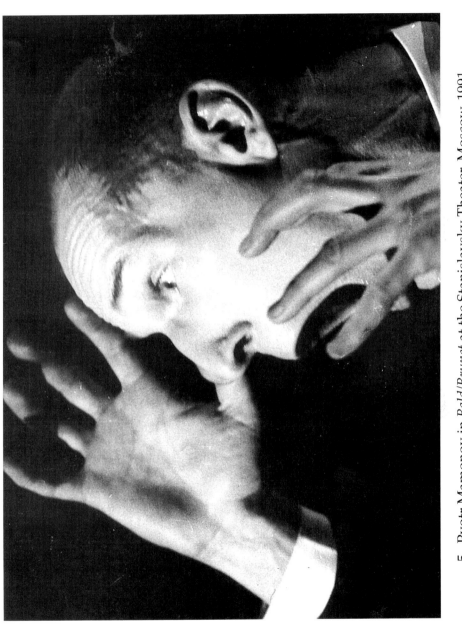

5. Pyotr Mamonov in *Bald/Brunet* at the Stanislavsky Theater, Moscow, 1991. (Photo: Mikhail Guterman)

6. Daniil Gink and daughter Masha. (Photo: Victor Bazhenov)

7. Daniil Gink. (Photo: Victor Bazhenov)

8. Oleg Menshikov (Nijinsky) and Alexander Feklistov (the Actor) in the Bogis Agency production of *Nijinsky*, Moscow, 1993. (Photo: the Bogis Agency)

9. Oleg Menshikov as Nijinsky in the Bogis Agency production of *Nijinsky*,
Moscow, 1993. (Photo: the Bogis Agency)

10. Alexander Feklistov as the Actor in the Bogis Agency production of
Nijinsky, Moscow, 1993. (Photo: the Bogis Agency)

11. Alexander Feklistov (the Actor) and Oleg Menshikov (Nijinsky) in the Bogis Agency production of *Nijinsky*, Moscow, 1993. (Photo: the Bogis Agency)

12. Oleg Menshikov (Nijinsky) and Alexander Feklistov (the Actor) in
the Bogis Agency production of *Nijinsky*, Moscow, 1993.
(Photo: Mikhail Guterman)

13. Alexei Burykin "hangs in the air at the top of a leap" in front of the Alexandrinsky Theater in St. Petersburg. (Photo: Oleg Menshikov)

14. Alexei Burykin in front of a drawing by Vaslav Nijinsky.
(Photo: Oleg Menshikov)

Nijinsky

A game of solitaire for two

By Alexei Burykin

A Few Words on the Entity that Is Nijinsky
(Author's Note)

Nijinsky is an improvized meeting between Genius and that Actor which every one of us is; an "eye-to-eye conversation—we certainly have met in the other world."

The Actor's thinking mechanism, though not uninventive, falters and ultimately grinds to a halt beneath the rush of those waves (rhythmic waves included) whose source is Nijinsky. My Nijinsky. The signature of genius, one is inclined to think, is distinguished by its list—it's all a matter of degrees. Nijinsky is the Actor's center of gravity; that spiritual burden which is not so easily revoked. (After Vaslav Nijinsky had long since abandoned the stage due to his diagnosis of "schizophrenia," Alexander Benois said of him: "That terrible sight arouses in me envy, not pity.")[1] However, the tormenting quest for understanding provides the Actor new moorings, insofar as poetry can be that. What remains is the sound of rain tapping out the rhythm of solitude.

These few words are not a cover letter for a perspicacious reader. More likely, they are a sketch without shadings.

Alexei Burykin

---

[1] I recommend that actors read Benois's entire letter to Sergei Diaghilev, dated December 28, 1928. I have quoted from it twice here.

DEDICATED TO OLEG MENSHIKOV

NIJINSKY: I love to speak in rhyme.
ACTOR: Does sir love poetry?
NIJINSKY: I am poetry.

NIJINSKY

CHARACTERS

NIJINSKY
AN ACTOR

ACT ONE

(Vaslav Nijinsky tumbles out on stage head over heels)

NIJINSKY. I'm free! I'm free! Those voices! I can't stand them! I can't take it anymore! *(Goes into a telephone booth, picks up the receiver and dials a number)* Hello, police? Help! Some maniac has been following me all morning! Evening? So what? What's that got to do with anything? You mean if I don't tell you, you're going to leave me unprotected? All alone? One on one maybe even with murderers? How should I know!? I'd be happy to tell you. But I don't see any street signs or store names. There's nothing. Except for this phone booth. The number? *(Erases the phone number)* I can't read it. I said, somebody completely erased it and I can't make it out. Same goes for you, buddy! You're more dangerous than my maniac. We haven't even made it to the Second Coming yet and you've already lost your mind! *(Humming gaily, he hangs up the phone. Dials another number)* Hello? Oh, what a velvety voice. Yes, yes. You know, I can tell what someone looks like just from their voice. You don't believe me? Hmm… You have blue eyes, a cute little nose, thin lips and a little dimple on your chin. Am I right? What charming laughter! Who are you, by the way? No, you tell me first. No, no, no… The fire station? I totally forgot! I called to tell you that I'm trapped in a raging fire. Where? All around me! Everything is consumed in flames. The whole world is trapped in a conflagration! Oh, yeah? Your voice changed. You have a disgusting figure and you're flat-chested! *(Hangs up the phone and hums happily. Dials a third number)* Hello, doctor? I'm dying. Of love. For mankind. That's not important. Listen to what I made up today. "God grant I don't go nuts!"[1] Thank you. Everything you know about the soul and the brain adds up to nothing. Less than nothing. Because there's nobody else to call! Oh, all right. Hey,

---

[1]This is an abomination of the first line of a famous poem by Alexander Pushkin. A literal translation of Pushkin's actual words: "God grant that I not lose my mind."

wait a second! I mean, you are a first aid service, aren't you? Quick, give me the number of the Central Public Whorehouse! I can't find it listed in the emergency section!

(Nijinsky hangs up the phone and leaves the booth, bumping into the Actor, who is carrying a small suitcase. Pause)

ACTOR. Got a match? I got separated from my lighter somewhere. Oh, that's right! You don't smoke! Basically, me neither. But sometimes, like whenever we meet, I can't help it. I mean, cigarettes are pure evil, but I can't do a damn thing about it. Too bad? Too bad! Too bad. Then it'll have to be a cigarette break without cigarettes. Kinda like music without sound or a play without words. But, we will be healthier, won't we? What's that? No, no, no. I have this thing against hotels. That's why I came straight to you. I thought through everything I have to say and I know all about your illness. I'm a big fan of peace and quiet. Just like you. *(Puts down his suitcase)* Have a seat.

(Nijinsky sits down)

Get up!

(Nijinsky doesn't move)

(The Actor holds out his hand) What's that? Rain? Here? I must have imagined it. *(Sits on his suitcase next to Nijinsky. Takes out a cigarette, a lighter and lights up)* I once was acquainted with… Well, not really acquainted, but during my rounds I used to run across a certain, you know, client who, were it not for certain alarming dreams, would have thought he was a king. Not of the world, mind you, but of endless space! The entire universe, so to speak. And you know, all he needed to convince him of that was to close himself up inside a nutshell. *(Laughs)* He was brutally betrayed and then they killed him. I think he was crucified.

(Actor locks a grip on Nijinsky, who doesn't react. The actor lifts Nijinsky's arm and turns his face to the side. Nijinsky remains in that pose)

And so, basically, all his dreams revolved around one thing. He kept getting on a train to go to his own funeral. How's that for a story? But then he'd realize he wasn't the one who had died. It was his name had died. Then he'd either stop the train or, in one of the other variants, he'd break out a window with his body and hurl himself out with the train still charging down the tracks, get up.

(Nijinsky stands up)

Lower your arm.

(Nijinsky drops his arm)

Or, maybe I got it all mixed up? Maybe there were two patients. I mean, clients. Maybe one had dreams and the other closed himself up in nutshells. Tell me prince, are you much of a ladies' man? *(Laughs)* I ask because just recently, by total coincidence, I ran into an old acquaintance. A remarkable lady. A striking brunette who is always in pants and a straw hat. She is simply crazy about athletics and athletes. You, uh, no? Yes? No? Well, it doesn't matter. That's the image you project. Naturally, she's not married. I recommend her highly. I'd be happy to relinquish her. Don't bother thanking me. *(Leans towards Nijinsky)* Or, perhaps brunettes aren't your type? *(Suddenly leaps up and starts racing around Nijinsky)* Then I'll find you a blonde or a red-head! Believe me, right here, backstage of life, there are more good-looking broads than you can shake a stick at! And if you're indifferent to the female sex in general, that's no problem either! *(Stops and wipes his brow with a bright handkerchief)* Whew! You do keep a pace! I can't keep up with you! What a pleasure that you're so silent. There's nothing boring about you! As the, uh, ancients used to say, "Silentium significare." Now, in the arts this very silentium is extraordinarily valuable, don't you think? "Stop the racket, won't you people? Let's recapture silentium primeval!" Splendid! However, my preferences lie elsewhere. Prepare yourself for a real blow. You see, of all the arts, I prefer the ballet. Do you enjoy the ballet? Isn't it a wonder? Not long ago I attended the debut of a totally unknown young dancer. My, but how he galloped across the stage! Frisky, gracious and handsome! But I just can't remember his name. It's one of those names, you know, a little like... Ah! I can't remember! They say they found him in the corps de ballet. How could I have forgotten that? I think it starts with an "m." Wait a minute! I have the program with me!

(Nijinsky falls off the suitcase. Pause)

Why so silent? You really don't think your silence will stop me on the road to truth? Believe me, nothing is simpler than reconstructing everything. Everything! Your labors, your liars *(gets carried away)* your loathers, your loonies, your lackeys, your loners, your losers. *(Suddenly snaps out of it)* My dear man, there are untold numbers who can easily testify to the truth about you. Do you hear me? The truth. About what happened wherever it was you really were. It's elementary. It's so easy.

(Nijinsky and the Actor speak simultaneously, paying no attention to one another)

NIJINSKY.	ACTOR.
I see through all.	It would be a hell of a job to find them all.
I don't need talk	And, to tell the truth, I don't have the money.
To grasp what's up:	Still, I'd hate to just give up on a tempting
I see through all.	idea like that. Maybe I'll take a different
They disagree:	tack. Go visit them all myself. Who cares
"You do not know him,	what it costs? It'd be worth it. But that
Or her or us,	wouldn't be very smart. To just drop you in
You cannot know me!"	a spot like this. They might even accuse me
I see through all.	of being a traitor. On the other hand, if
I see the truth	you're going to be pig-headed…
In deeds uncouth.	
As plain as that.	
What's that you say?	

ACTOR. What did you say? I'm not joking. By the way, it was a coincidence brought me to you. Not even a coincidence, really, a fluke. I'll tell you about it later. You'll get a kick out of it! It's a great story with a real fantastic flair! However, from the point of view of our little case, so to speak, the most important thing is for you to calm down. No nerves. No stress. I'm going to help you get back on your feet. How's your diet? What medicines are you taking? Do you sleep well? Are you bothered by nightmares? How about voices? And, finally, how are your bowel movements? Relax and close your eyes. Shut them, I said! We'll take care of this all by ourselves. Now, imagine a seashore caressed in sunlight. The scent of seaweed, the cry of sea gulls, the rustle of waves and surf, the sea, the sea…

(Nijinsky leaps up and begins running around the Actor, roaring)

Hey! What are you doing? I came to… How are you going to hear sea sounds? Calm down! I am your friend! I came to help you! Why upset yourself like this? What are you doing?! *(Running out)* Wait right there! I'll be right back! Only… You won't even be able to count to sixty, and I'll be back. *(Disappears)* No more than sixty!

(Nijinsky stops running. He opens the Actor's suitcase. It is empty. Nijinsky's vision of his parents, Tomasz and Eleonora)

NIJINSKY.
  Flesh and dust—
  Threat and fear!

Shall I disappear? Or shall I let him in?
Or, maybe, kick him out of here! But without
Your word—bereft of your consent—
I know I'm doomed to
Shouts
And screams
And bitter discontent!
Now, here I am! I'm whole again!

TOMASZ NIJINSKY.
  To break and sunder fate, my son, that is my art.
  Don't waste your time: evil brooks each glancing blow.
  Don't copy me. Allow for all to be and then
  Seek to forgive. Find peace in your own heart.
  Live a king unto yourself. Why disavow
  Your solitude, and thereby violate those laws
  You make yourself? I swear:
  Nowhere will you find a crueler lot in this drab life.

ELEONORA NIJINSKA.
  How can I describe
  My shapeless fears in words?
  My speech has died.
  My sounds are poor.
  I cannot say it right!
  O son, dear boy,
  Safeguard your precious life!
  Danger, pass him by!
  Shield my boy from shame!
  Show him love, not hate!
  Spare him pain!

NIJINSKY.
  The circle is complete. And now
  My goal's to leap from it!
  I need an out.
  I know this guest before me represents
  The universal aggregate,
  But where's the out?
  Does a duel with this pretense
  Have any chance of making sense?

(The Actor runs in holding a straight-jacket. He doesn't see Nijinsky)

ACTOR. *(Indecisively)* Now, I got y... Hey! Where are you? Ha-ll-oo! Come out, come out, wherever you are! I won't hurt you... You just can't turn your back on him! Where did he disappear to? Weird, weird, weird... There's no way... Where could he have gone to? He's gone! He's gone! Well then, here goes. It's all or nothing! *(Flips a coin)* I'm either a prince or a pauper! *(Catches the coin and looks at it with satisfaction)* Aha! Call me a prince! All right, then... *(Begins looking for Nijinsky)*

NIJINSKY.
My Lord! What grace and wonder —
Renouncing people and the words
They speak! Breaking free
Of gods! Sensing musical vibrations
With every fiber of the body!
Silence! Silence! Silence!
To softly blend with Nothing, Nil and Never,
In the mirror of mirages!

(The Actor spreads his arms and shrugs his shoulders. Flips a coin again, catches it, looks at it)

ACTOR. Bah!
NIJINSKY. One minute, thirty-seven seconds.
ACTOR. *(Startled)* What?
NIJINSKY. Is that how you keep your word?
ACTOR. What do you mean?
NIJINSKY. I counted up to ninety-seven.
ACTOR. So what?
NIJINSKY. You didn't keep your word!
ACTOR. I didn't give my...
NIJINSKY. You promised to return promptly in one minute.
ACTOR. *(Finally gathering his wits)* Obviously, you should have counted more slowly. Where were you?
NIJINSKY. In Kiev. That's where I was born. During Shrovetide. That day I received my first-ever gift from my father when I was just a few hours old.

(The Actor fumbles with a straight-jacket, pretending he's paying no attention to Nijinsky)

My father was a better dancer than I. But he was a drunk and never accomplished anything. The last time we saw each other, he gave me some cuff links made out of stones from the Ural Mountains. I remember him standing on the dock. He was waving a blue handkerchief at the steamer I was leaving on. I never saw my father again.

ACTOR. What about your mother?

NIJINSKY. I learned to walk, talk and dance all at the same time, and my mother—who kept track of every new tooth I got—would never be able to say when I had my first dance lesson.

(Pause)

ACTOR. Please, go on.

NIJINSKY. The family disintegrated. My brother died…

ACTOR. In a madhouse!

NIJINSKY. Yes, I had just turned…

ACTOR. Eight-teen-years-old.

(Pause)

NIJINSKY. We always liked each other. And I loved working with my sister. She always understood my slightest gesture. For a long time I had no news about either her or my mother. The absence of information for several years was terribly painful. Then I just didn't care anymore.

(Pause)

ACTOR. Yes, yes, yes, yes, yes! It's the absence of information that determines our actions, isn't it? But what about your daughter?

NIJINSKY. I was enraptured by her singing. She would sing like this—"ah-ah-ah-ah"—and I was happy. Because it meant that everything is joyous and nothing is terrible. As for my son, things were more complex…

ACTOR. You mean you had a son?

NIJINSKY. I know very little about him. He hasn't been born yet.

ACTOR. I see. You have been through a lot, haven't you, sir? May I call you "sir"? But you should know I truly want to help you.

NIJINSKY. *(Becoming animated)* Really? Are you rich?

ACTOR. *(After a pause)* How much do you need?

NIJINSKY. I know money is a filthy thing, but I need some badly in order to undermine the World Stock Exchange. I'm going to make money on its collapse!

ACTOR. Undermine the World Stock Exchange?! What do you mean? What for?

NIJINSKY. Death! The World Stock Exchange represents death! But I will win and God will help me.

ACTOR. *(Taking out a check book)* Well, I am indebted to you for saving me a good deal of trouble. How much do you need? Don't be shy.

NIJINSKY. Couldn't you make it in cash?

ACTOR. Sorry, but I don't have much with me. I'm afraid it wouldn't be enough to get you a taxi ride... *(sniggers)* down to the World Stock Exchange.

NIJINSKY. Don't worry. I've got two-hundred and fifteen francs of my own hidden away.

ACTOR. Two-hundred francs...

NIJINSKY. Two-hundred and fifteen!

ACTOR. What do you need money for? Let's just imagine that you amass an enormous sum on the market—although the market isn't a game of roulette, you know.

NIJINSKY. I am convinced I will win, because I am life.

ACTOR. *(After a pause)* And what are you planning to do with your earnings?

NIJINSKY. I'm thinking about going to a bordello.

ACTOR. You're thinking about going where?

NIJINSKY. I know it sounds crazy, but I always wanted to learn more about the psychological make-up of prostitutes. I'll take on a couple...

(The Actor grunts in surprise)

I get overwhelmed by an amazing sexual excitement and a terrible fear at the same time. Blood rushes to my head and I'm afraid I'm going to have a stroke. But if that's what God wants, then I'll give the women all my money for free. I won't ask them for anything.

ACTOR. How gauche! That's despicable!

NIJINSKY. Despicable? Of me? I hate despicable acts. *(Pause)* And if I've ever done anything despicable, it's only because at that moment I was blinded to the presence of God in my soul.

ACTOR. Listen, what right do you have to talk about God in the same breath with bordellos?

NIJINSKY. Hmm... Do you happen to wear a monocle?

ACTOR. Pardon me?

NIJINSKY. A mo-no-cle.

ACTOR. No. I do not wear a monocle. I only wear glasses when reading.

NIJINSKY. What do you usually read? Public relations prospecti?

ACTOR. Words, words, words...

NIJINSKY. So, do you refuse to give me a loan?

ACTOR. No. What are you worried about? Of course I'll give you a loan. You've got me all confused. Is the good sir serious or is he making fun?

NIJINSKY. The good sir is serious! *(He suddenly grabs the Actor)*

ACTOR. What are you doing?

NIJINSKY. Shhh!

ACTOR. What is going on?

NIJINSKY. Quiet! I hate people bothering me when I'm working.
ACTOR. Working? *(Explodes)* What are you doing, for God's sake!?

(Pause)

NIJINSKY. I am a master at reading expressions. I can tell a liar just by looking at his face.
ACTOR. *(Wiping off his face with a handkerchief)* What am I, pray tell?
NIJINSKY. Let me give you some advice: Dedicate your money to love.
ACTOR. Are you saying I'm a liar?
NIJINSKY. Love is the oldest word!
ACTOR. So, who am I? Who am I? Who do you think I am? Who am I?
NIJINSKY. Life is not sex and sex is not God.
ACTOR. Oh for Christ's sake, would you quit invoking the Lord's name everywhere you shouldn't be? Quit playing the parrot: God, God, God!
NIJINSKY. *(Suddenly angering)* Aha! So it's you, then! You were always sneaking around behind my back! You think I'm afraid of you? Get out of my sight! You were always hiding out and sneaking around keeping an eye on me! I didn't invite you! And I don't need your filthy money! They sent you to kill me, didn't they? To destroy my life. It won't work! Get out! Get out of here! I suspected you from the very start! The air itself quivered when you came in here. I could feel it constrict my throat. But God wants me to stay. And as for the errors I have committed, I, more than anyone, have redeemed myself through my life and my suffering!
ACTOR. *(Shouts)* Name! Whose name shall I make the check out to? Come on! First name! Last name! Be quick about it!
NIJINSKY. No, no. I don't know. No, no, no.

(A long pause)

ACTOR. Well then, do you know the exact amount you need to get your game started? Don't refuse my money, because, as I understand it, God himself is sending you off to the World Stock Exchange. And who else is going to help you besides me?

(Nijinsky is silent)

You see?
NIJINSKY. *(Softly)* Y-e-s, I suppose you're right. Everything is just as you say. Forgive me, please. I wasn't being fair.
ACTOR. Oh, let's cut the sentiment. So…
NIJINSKY. I really don't know how much I need exactly.
ACTOR. Here are a thousand francs. Go on, take it. *(Offers Nijinsky the money)*

NIJINSKY. Thank you very much. You are a very noble and a very cunning person. I accept this money from you as a loan and I will immediately go down to...

ACTOR. Immediately?

NIJINSKY. I would ask you to step out. A change of clothes is in order. I have many very nice suits, travelling suits included.

ACTOR. But it's nighttime.

NIJINSKY. Are you sure about that?

ACTOR. Well, everything is relative of course.

NIJINSKY. Perhaps, in truth, it is evening. Or, for example, morning. Last evening I saw Mars and it was absolutely uninhabited. I know this planet well, although I am not under its influence. And you?

ACTOR. What? Mars? You mean "that planet covered in ice, which, one million years ago, was just like our planet Earth, and which risks a similar fate if no one listens to me"—that is, you, of course—"and if no one closes all the factories"? Uh! Did I quote you properly?

NIJINSKY. Yes, yes, that's the planet. Nobody ever paid any attention to me! If God had ordered me to go, I would have done what Tolstoy did in his time. He ran away from his wife. I read his books and it always seemed to me I understood him. He wanted to save the Earth, too.

ACTOR. But you, where would you go, sir?

NIJINSKY. Oh, my political platform is extraordinarily simple. It merely consists in being at one with the entire world.

ACTOR. *(Smiles)* Are you able to do that?

NIJINSKY. What?

ACTOR. Are you able to be at one with me?

NIJINSKY. Don't laugh, you miserable cur! What I want to know is, what are you doing here? I was wrong! They were right! Don't touch me! Don't even come near me! How can you go anywhere in shoes like that? Can't you see what they look like? That's disgusting—to come bursting in here in filthy shoes like that! Maybe you're right. Maybe it is nighttime, but don't expect a farewell handshake from me! I wouldn't even consider touching a person in shoes like that!

ACTOR. What about my story? Don't you want to hear my story?

NIJINSKY. What story?

ACTOR. The one that brought me to you. I was out taking a walk...

NIJINSKY. I don't care about your story.

ACTOR. ...the sun was shining on the shrubbery...

NIJINSKY. I've got enough stories of my own.

ACTOR. ...and suddenly I noticed blood...

NIJINSKY. I am inundated in stories like... What? What did you notice?

ACTOR. Blood on the grass. A tiny trail of bloody spots.

NIJINSKY. And then what?

ACTOR. I followed the trail.

NIJINSKY. The what?

ACTOR. The trail.

NIJINSKY. Why did you follow the trail?

ACTOR. You know, I don't really know. But the sight of blood, somehow, just attracts attention.

NIJINSKY. I see.

ACTOR. Uh, I started walking around the woods, like a real sleuth bloodhound, until I came upon a precipice. And at the very brink, the trail broke off. I leaned over to look and—you wouldn't believe it!—there wasn't anybody there.

NIJINSKY. Who did you think you'd see?

(Pause)

ACTOR. Maybe a person... But you know what amazed me more than anything? This was the real killer. When I turned around—you won't believe it!—instead of blood, there was a pile of goat manure! Imagine that! All that time I had been fooling myself, following a false trail. I don't know if my imagination just got the better of me or if I suffered a sun stroke. But the reality was plain to see: goat manure! Nature is the greatest genius! I burst out laughing and went back to my hotel.

NIJINSKY. The same thing happened with me!

ACTOR. That's just what I wanted to verify.

NIJINSKY. Only, I was moved by God's will and it was winter.

ACTOR. Winter, was it?

NIJINSKY. Yes. I followed the trail of blood, fully convinced that this was the place where the murder had taken place. I stopped at the edge of the precipice and looked down. And, in fact, there was no one there.

ACTOR. Goat manure instead of blood!

NIJINSKY. I'm no biologist. All I knew was that God was testing me. On my way back, I shouted, "I fear Thee not! Thou art Life, not Death!" Suddenly, I saw blood in the snow again. That's when I got angry.

ACTOR. You were, so to speak, beside yourself?

NIJINSKY. Yes, on occasion I step out of my... I mean, I escape... But He said to me, "Stop!" and I stopped. "Stop reasoning," and I stopped. I stood there so long my hands started aching from the cold. And then I heard His voice one more time: "Go!" He said to me. And I went.

ACTOR. Were you alone?

NIJINSKY. *(With irritation)* I already told you!

ACTOR. All right, all right, all right. Only, why all these intricate fabrications?

NIJINSKY. This is all very close to me. It could never have happened to you! You're just a silly fool who turned what happened to me into a joke. The only thing that has any significance in reality is whatever God commands.

ACTOR. I presume God will not be insisting on the committing of any murders?

They both stare at one another)

NIJINSKY. *(After a pause)* I looked through the evening papers and, while I don't know German, English, Italian or Hungarian, they are all accessible to my understanding. And I understood that there had been no murder. French, a little bit.

ACTOR. And so, it was winter.

NIJINSKY. Or, maybe summer.

ACTOR. *(Sarcastically)* How about autumn?

NIJINSKY. Or spring. I know you don't believe me, but I'm not angry with you. I absolve even my murderer of everything. Goodbye.

ACTOR. Are you kicking me out?

NIJINSKY. Why is it that I always have to explain to anyone and everyone why I want to be left alone with myself?!

ACTOR. I'm not just anyone. And anyway, I think you're better off not remaining in such dangerous company.

NIJINSKY. That's none of your business. Farewell.

ACTOR. What about your trip?

NIJINSKY. What trip?

ACTOR. *(Grinning)* To the World Stock Exchange.

NIJINSKY. I just received a telegram. I've been invited to Paris. To perform…

ACTOR. *(Interrupting him)* Who invited you?

NIJINSKY. I have to get myself ready.

ACTOR. May I have a peek?

NIJINSKY. Why should I have to lean on the printed word to prove what I said?

ACTOR. That's not the point. *(Snatches the telegram from Nijinsky)*

NIJINSKY. *(In confusion)* I will not tolerate anyone messing in my affairs! I don't need an impresario!

ACTOR. There is a date here. March 9, 1914. When was that?

(Pause)

NIJINSKY. I can see by my never-failing watch that it's time for you to go. And please do have a shoeshine boy clean your shoes!

ACTOR. What do you want to know the psychology of prostitutes for?

NIJINSKY. What?

ACTOR. You led me to believe that you are interested in the psychology of prostitutes. I can offer you several brochures on the topic. It makes for fascinating research!

NIJINSKY. Who did the research?

ACTOR. I did!

NIJINSKY. You? What do you have to do with it?

ACTOR. I'd like to ask you the same thing.

NIJINSKY. It's crucial for me, because I... When I was... Uh, weren't you just about on your way out?

ACTOR. Curiosity kept me here. Now, you were saying—when you were...

(Pause. Nijinsky takes off a shoe and throws it at the Actor, who ducks)

NIJINSKY. Excuse me, but I had no other choice. God ordered me to do that.

ACTOR. And what if God... orders you to kill? Me, for example. What will you do?

NIJINSKY. I will obey him. *(Takes off his other shoe, throws it at the Actor, hitting him squarely)*

ACTOR. This is not farewell. *(Disappears)*

(Nijinsky's visions: his wife Romola Pulska, and Sergei Diaghilev)

ROMOLA PULSKA.
  Don't worship him! He poisoned you.
  And ever since, his iron grip
  Won't let you slip away.
  You do not owe him fame,
  His stamp is shame.
  And I, for evermore, will be your slave.

NIJINSKY.
  That's a pretty tune! What say we play
  A little game, a double comedy?
  Who now is in the suit of prostitute?
  Dance married us. Hear that?
  The music plays! The time is up!
  Your cue! Let's cancel all the gossip!

ROMOLA PULSKA.
  O, dance! A hymn to flesh and prancing
  Life! A simpleton could never understand the
  Dance! A wild, writhing path
  That leads the heart into an avalanche
  Of earthly passions!
  Dance, thanks to you...
  I thank you, Dance!

SERGEI DIAGHILEV.
  Prancing life? Whose lips
  Have uttered that? Your hissing,
  Lisping voice bears naught but death.
  Until you shut your trap no one shall ever
  Understand the soothing sounds
  Of him so pure… The heavens themselves
  Would sooner crack, you snake, than you
  Admit: The blame is all your own!

ROMOLA PULSKA.
  I must say, dear man, your fitful gust
  Is nothing more than empty fuss.

SERGEI DIAGHILEV.
  You lie. It hurts!
  Say now: Did you
  Not steal him,
  Tricking me by hunting out
  My weakness?
  And did you not, my friend, with your own hand
  Effect his plummet from the heights
  Back to oblivion?

ROMOLA PULSKA.
  Oh, but how I love him!
  I am his pulse, his extra sense.
  And you are fear, the persecuting fear of misery.
  You know the art
  Of burning others in yourself and turning them to ashes!
  You love…

SERGEI DIAGHILEV.
  Enough.

ROMOLA PULSKA.
  You love…

SERGEI DIAGHILEV.
  Enough!

ROMOLA PULSKA.
  You love another now!

SERGEI DIAGHILEV.
  Enough, I say!!!

ROMOLA PULSKA.
  I love it when he hurts so much,
  When he can't bear to look me in the eye.

NIJINSKY.
  I am the bone of contention; the arrow
  Striking to the marrow of the human soul,
  In hopes of splitting open that ripe
  Fruit. Yes, we know that good remains
  The eternal root of evil.
  How silly are their efforts!
  The picture of pure madness!
  No matter how you spin it,
  Virtue ever runs in step beside the Devil.

(Enter the Actor in a woman's make-up)

ACTOR. I welcome you on behalf of the Central Public Whorehouse!
  Reservation number double-0, 0, 0, one. Privacy is guaranteed.
NIJINSKY. Let me get a better look at your face. Come closer.
ACTOR. You don't think I'm trying to deceive you?
NIJINSKY. I should warn you. Everyone everywhere *(hesitates)* considered
  me insane.
ACTOR. You don't say!
NIJINSKY. I'll tell you a little secret.
ACTOR. I adore other people's secrets!
NIJINSKY. I don't like to be around people or among grown-ups. I don't
  know how. The only thing I like is to be with children.
ACTOR. Our institution is not equipped to help you with that. Farewell.
NIJINSKY. Farewell.
ACTOR. *(Offended)* I am so young! One might even say unsullied!
NIJINSKY. Answer one question.
ACTOR. Money up front.
NIJINSKY. Money is evil.
ACTOR. That's my business. If you get what I mean.
NIJINSKY. I'll teach you how to use make-up.
ACTOR. What's wrong with mine?
NIJINSKY. You have to transform yourself from within. Turn yourself
  completely into another being. You don't have what it takes for that.
ACTOR. *(Wiping off his make-up)* Why? I can try.

NIJINSKY. *(Harshly)* Tell me immediately! How far is it to the sun?

ACTOR. How should I know?

NIJINSKY. I'll kill you.

ACTOR. *(Quickly)* 150 million kilometers.

NIJINSKY. How about to the moon? Come on.

ACTOR. Three hundred and eighty-five thousand. What the hell are you driving at?

NIJINSKY. Both, to tell you the truth.

ACTOR. Is that so? Allow me to introduce myself: Sergei Pavlovich Diaghilev. Vaslav, my dear boy, don't you recognize me? How have you been?

NIJINSKY. *(In disgust)* Don't try taking him on. That's no role for you.

ACTOR. Do you remember that hotel?

NIJINSKY. Drop him, I said!

ACTOR. We had just been introduced and you were so weak…

NIJINSKY. *(Aloofly)* I fainted.

ACTOR. Yes! You just plopped on the floor. I was so afraid for you that I called the doctor.

NIJINSKY. The doctor found nothing wrong and you brought me an orange.

ACTOR. I took your hand in mine…

NIJINSKY. *(Suddenly)* I was out of money! How many times do I have to tell you? I need pocket change for minor expenses! I can't be bothered with that every moment of the day!

ACTOR. *(In confusion)* But I… I gave you a thousand francs. That's all I had with me.

NIJINSKY. I need two thousand francs by tomorrow. And I have no desire to wait any longer! I am a free man and I do as I please!

ACTOR. Of course, of course. But who pays your bills?

NIJINSKY. I don't need support like that! I want my own money and I want to spend it however I want. You don't even allow me the most basic needs.

ACTOR. What do you consider the most "basic needs?" Where did you go last night, just to spite me?

NIJINSKY. I didn't do anything to spite you! Yesterday, the day before yesterday, or the day before the day before yesterday. I'm sick of constantly being followed.

ACTOR. You can do anything your heart desires.

NIJINSKY. I'm not talking about the ballet. How come the sheets aren't changed more often? Tell them I want the bed changed every morning!

ACTOR. What are you talking about? Vasily is in charge of that.

NIJINSKY Vasily follows me! Get him away from me! I see his disgusting face everywhere I go!

ACTOR. A face no worse than any other.

NIJINSKY. A mug.
ACTOR. A face.
NIJINSKY. A mug!
ACTOR. A face!

(Long pause)

NIJINSKY. Now comes the blow with the walking cane. Like this! *(Hits the Actor)*
ACTOR. *(Shocked)* What are you doing? That hurts.
NIJINSKY. It hurts me, too.
ACTOR. You scum! *(Flies at Nijinsky, begins beating him)* You scoundrel! You liar! Do you know who you are? You're a two-bit hoofer, that's who! Your madness is hereditary. And if you hadn't made such a huge, mysterious legend out of it, you would have been nothing but fine print in a ballet encyclopedia. The only time anybody would ever remember you would be when some teacher in a kid's ballet school was showing some kid how to jump! You're an ape! *(Walks away)*

(Long pause)

NIJINSKY. I wonder whether we are nothing but lonely rhythms?
ACTOR. Shut up. I'm asking the questions, and you're answering. You got that?
NIJINSKY. When?
ACTOR. What do you mean, when? Now! Now! Now! I'm asking you: Is that clear?
NIJINSKY. Is that already the first question?
ACTOR. Don't get smart with me!
NIJINSKY. I need time to collect myself. It's been ages since I gave an interview.
ACTOR. What can I do to help? Pop you in the face?
NIJINSKY. Very funny. All right, I get you.
ACTOR. What?
NIJINSKY. *(Making faces)* You... are going... to ask... questions... and I... am going... to answer. Question, answer. Question, answer. Question...

(The Actor slaps Nijinsky)

ACTOR. Idiot!
NIJINSKY. Now that's a whole different story. Only I have to say interviewers are usually better behaved. But, comparisons can be quite illuminating.

ACTOR. Are you finished? And now…

NIJINSKY. I don't like your being so familiar with me!

ACTOR. *(Threateningly)* And now!

NIJINSKY. I will not tolerate that tone!

ACTOR. *(Angrily)* And now!!!

NIJINSKY. *(Shouts)* Where is my lawyer?

ACTOR. *(Shouts)* What do you think God is?

NIJINSKY. *(Not hesitating)* God is a human being who fertilizes a woman and from that one and only woman he begets children.

(Pause)

ACTOR. You… What?

NIJINSKY. I don't know.

ACTOR. You mean you seriously believe that God is a human being? And specifically, a man? Any healthy man?

NIJINSKY. God is God. And human beings came from God, not from apes. And apes came from apes who were created by God.

ACTOR. Wait, wait, wait! I didn't ask you about apes. And so, God is the power capable of producing…

NIJINSKY. Love.

ACTOR. What did you say?

NIJINSKY. Love and nothing more.

ACTOR. You are not listening to me!

NIJINSKY. On the contrary. People usually say that humans are born from the seed of the father in the womb of the mother. But I am saying that the seed descends not from the first human, but from God himself. A human is flesh and feeling. If a human is made of flesh, then that's what he comes from.

ACTOR. What you are saying is that humans develop like apes.

NIJINSKY. In fact, it's just the opposite. It was God who created flesh. The similarity between humans and apes is purely organic and has nothing to do with spirituality. God is not an ape and a human is a part of God.

ACTOR. So. Let's begin from the beginning. You say that God is a human being?

NIJINSKY. Life.

ACTOR. In that case, it follows that good and bad are the essence of God.

NIJINSKY. My God is the God of good. However, I can't be responsible for a bad person.

ACTOR. Aha! You mean that there are many different manifestations of God in the world!

NIJINSKY. I wish you no evil, but my wife's father committed suicide because he thought too much. Believe me, I wish evil upon no one! And my mind is not damaged.

ACTOR. What does your mind have to do with it?

NIJINSKY. Absolutely nothing. People used to say about Diaghilev that he didn't have a single sou but his mind was worth an entire fortune. I don't have any money either and I'm not very smart, but I have a soul.

ACTOR. I have a soul, too!

NIJINSKY. You see? And you keep talking about apes! I hate polemics. Silence is the best tactic in any argument.

(Pause. The Actor is on the verge of saying something, but Nijinsky stops him with a gesture. Pause)

ACTOR. *(Carefully)* What happened?

NIJINSKY. *(Standing motionlessly)* I dance.

(Pause)

ACTOR. Wait a minute! You say that God…

NIJINSKY. *(Interrupting harshly)* What do you want?

ACTOR. Wait, wait, wait, wait! I'm the one asking questions.

NIJINSKY. I'm tired of you.

ACTOR. That's not funny. Now, listen. Listen very carefully! Whoever He may be, God only exists apart from humans, right? Isn't that so? I'm asking you: Isn't that so?

NIJINSKY. *(Speaking at a break-neck speed without pauses)* I am a human a human and God I am a red-skinned Indian a black man an Egyptian a foreigner an alien a Chinaman I am the God of any living creature I am a sea bird and the bird above the land I am a bear a bison a dolphin…

ACTOR. Shut up.

NIJINSKY. …I am a peasant a worker a prince a king I am a contemporary of Shakespeare Pushkin Wagner Bach I am earth fire air water motion and life wisdom and feeling…

ACTOR. *(Grasping his head)* Shut up!! I demand that you shut up!

NIJINSKY. …I am Buddha I am Christ the spirit in flesh and flesh in spirit I am a butterfly I am a flower I am a man and a woman I am one whole I am anywhere and everywhere I am love and eternity I I I I…

(The Actor seizes a bottle of cognac and, after clasping Nijinsky's head firmly between his knees, empties out half of the bottle. Nijinsky immediately goes limp and topples on the floor. The Actor takes a sip from the bottle. Pause)

ACTOR. Now I understand. You belong in a museum of oddities. I'll marinate you and send you to Zurich. *(Laughs)* Or to Paris. Or, maybe, London. You'll be right at home with all those two-headed freaks and hermaphrodites! They'll give you your own shelf with your own name-tag on which they'll write…

NIJINSKY. *(Interrupting)* Good cognac.
ACTOR. What?
NIJINSKY. *(Leaping up in one deft motion)* Shh!
ACTOR. What?
NIJINSKY. Shhh!
ACTOR. Quit goofing off!
NIJINSKY. *(Insistently)* Shush!

(The Actor freezes and listens carefully. Pause)

ACTOR. *(Whispering)* What's going on?
NIJINSKY. That moment will never happen again. Ne-ver.
ACTOR. It's always like that.
NIJINSKY. Particularly here.
ACTOR. Especially here.
NIJINSKY. I have to warn you of impending danger. *(Takes the bottle from the Actor, takes a sip and gives it back)* If measures aren't taken, it will be too late.

(A puzzled look comes over the Actor's face)

I see how you suffer. It's because you theorize too much. My wife theorized a lot, too. And you know what that led to. I gather you eat meat?
ACTOR. *(Decisively)* I don't see the connection.
NIJINSKY. Connections are always invisible. You can only sense them intuitively. For example, I can see without looking. Can you?
ACTOR. How do you do that?
NIJINSKY. Eyes aren't all you need to see objects or people's actions.
ACTOR. Liar!
NIJINSKY. I help myself through feeling. The blind understand me perfectly. The blind and the mad. They are the ones I communicate with.
ACTOR. Ha! It sounds to me like you're theorizing, yourself.
NIJINSKY. No, I'm telling you that I feel. And anyway, you're the one who started all this.
ACTOR. Me? I am but the consequence. You are the cause.
NIJINSKY. The cause is in God.
ACTOR. There you go again!
NIJINSKY. There are times when it even seems that all those who live in me actually exist independently. All on their own. But I can't verify that. How could you verify that?

(The Actor drinks from the bottle)

ACTOR. I remember ab-solute-ly nothing!

NIJINSKY. Fool.
ACTOR. Take that back.
NIJINSKY. Loof. You're a phony.
ACTOR. *(Stubbornly)* Take that back!
NIJINSKY. I can't.
ACTOR. Why?
NIJINSKY. Because you are neither blind nor mad.
ACTOR. No, I'm mad.
NIJINSKY. No you're not.
ACTOR. Yes I am!
NIJINSKY. No you're not!
ACTOR. All right then! I'm blind.

(Nijinsky carefully looks over the Actor)

NIJINSKY. *(After a pause)* Yes, you're blind. However, you can see. That means your blindness isn't real.
ACTOR. What is it, then?
NIJINSKY. You don't lose your sight just because I call you blind. That's not the point.
ACTOR. What is the point?
NIJINSKY. I already told you.
ACTOR. No you didn't.
NIJINSKY. Yes I did.
ACTOR. No you didn't.
NIJINSKY. Yes I did.
ACTOR. Well, in that case, I wasn't satisfied with what you said! Basically, you haven't given me a single satisfactory answer to any one of my questions!
NIJINSKY. On top of everything else, you're deaf!
ACTOR. *(Happily)* There! You see how useful it is to theorize? Now I know who I am.
NIJINSKY. Who are you?
ACTOR. *(Offended)* I'm not saying.
NIJINSKY. Is that so?
ACTOR. That's right! What's it to you?
NIJINSKY. Do you have a name?
ACTOR. What of it?
NIJINSKY. Names create fates.
ACTOR. Fates create names.
NIJINSKY. Or the other way around.
ACTOR. *(Shaking his head in agreement)* Yeah, or the other way around. *(Drinks some cognac)* But I still can't figure out whether you're faking or not.

NIJINSKY. Faking.
ACTOR. Aha!

(Both grab for the bottle)

NIJINSKY. Thoughts are useless if they aren't dangerous. That's why I don't like Hamlet. He's always theorizing instead of trusting his feelings.
ACTOR. I can't stand Hamlet either! *(Sobbing)* Maybe I was a blind man and now I can see?
NIJINSKY. Maybe. Only that was a long time ago. You are very sick. All of you. You poor, sick star. *(Drinks)*

(The Actor weeps)

Only don't act like a woman. They're always crying. Knock it off. *(Removes a handkerchief from the Actor's pocket and wipes his face with it)*

ACTOR. *(Sobbing)* Don't you ever cry?
NIJINSKY. All the time. But even if they plucked out my eyes, I would still be able to cry, because my tears flow in my soul. What would you do if they plucked out your eyes?
ACTOR. Knock it off!

(Nijinsky gets up)

(Severely) You just wait.

(Nijinsky stops)

Take back what you said.
NIJINSKY. About what?
ACTOR. What?
NIJINSKY. What specifically?
ACTOR. Everything. You hear me? Everything! Everything! Everything!

(Nijinsky leaves. The Actor drinks from the nearly-empty bottle and laughs)

That's it. That's enough. I quit this game! I've got to... at least see my partner. What is going on? First he's here and then he's gone! What is... *(Gets confused)* Hands up! *(Raises his hand)* I'm arrested. For life. *(Laughs)* Let somebody else finish out the game. I've had it!

(Nijinsky peers out)

NIJINSKY. Hey you! Nameless!
ACTOR. Huh?
NIJINSKY. I thought about it and did it.
ACTOR. Did what?
NIJINSKY. Took it back. All of it. *(Disappears)*

(The Actor roars violently)

ACTOR. Now wait a minute! If I don't... then who will? We are still... *(Gives himself commands, fulfilling them uncertainly)* Ab-out face! Hut, two... *(Falls. Gets up)* Try it again. Ab-out face! Hut, two, there you go. *(Drinks the last of the cognac and tosses the bottle away)* Take it from the top. Ab-out face! *(Disappears up stage)*

END OF ACT ONE

ACT TWO

(Nijinsky alone)

NIJINSKY.
 I am here and there,
 Imagination everywhere,
 A shimmering reflection
 Of a lost, wayfaring face.
 I am here and there. Snared
 In a magical game of my own making,
 I am the talk of the town
 On earth as in heaven!
 I am everywhere! I sparkle, I hide,
 I will always return
 'Til the day the world, love and I
 Shall plunge into oblivion!

(Enter the Actor)

ACTOR. First name, middle name, last name?

(Nijinsky is silent)

 Date of birth?
NIJINSKY. Eighteen eighty-nine.
ACTOR. Aha! Or was it 1890?
NIJINSKY. I don't remember.
ACTOR. Place of birth?
NIJINSKY. Kiev.
ACTOR. Or was it Warsaw?
NIJINSKY. I was baptized in Warsaw.
ACTOR. What do you love most in the world?
NIJINSKY. Lobster.
ACTOR. What do you hate?
NIJINSKY. Myself.
ACTOR. Your favorite subject?
NIJINSKY. My comb.
ACTOR. Color?
NIJINSKY. Lilac.
ACTOR. Flower?
NIJINSKY. Rose.
ACTOR. Don't lie!

NIJINSKY. Sorry. Baobab.

ACTOR. That's not a flower!

NIJINSKY. The baobab blossoms once a year. For one night. In June.

ACTOR. February.

NIJINSKY. June!

ACTOR. All right. In June if it's June. Favorite book?

NIJINSKY. The Idiot.

ACTOR. To whom are you referring?

NIJINSKY. Dostoevsky. The Idiot.

ACTOR. The Idiot. Dostoevsky. All right. Your most treasured dream?

NIJINSKY. To forget everything.

ACTOR. You mean, everything?

NIJINSKY. Sometimes you remind me of a dinosaur.

ACTOR. Don't try avoiding an answer.

NIJINSKY. What was the question?

ACTOR. Shall I repeat it?

(Pause)

Well?

NIJINSKY. Well, what?

ACTOR. All right, let's go on. Your ideal?

NIJINSKY. Magic.

ACTOR. That's an answer to another question.

NIJINSKY. Which one?

ACTOR. Are you tired or are you faking?

NIJINSKY. No good! By the way, who are you?

ACTOR. *(Laughing)* Napoleon!

NIJINSKY. Where did you come from?

ACTOR. A funeral.

NIJINSKY. Mine?

ACTOR. What do you think?

NIJINSKY. Tell me about it.

ACTOR. There's nothing to tell. I don't even know where to begin.

NIJINSKY. I know what you mean. I've been buried so many times, I myself don't know how many times I've been buried. In honor of my death they staged benefit concerts, learned lectures and gala balls! Only they didn't invite me. But let me give you some help.

ACTOR. How?

NIJINSKY. For example. Was everyone in mourning?

ACTOR. Almost.

NIJINSKY. How about flowers? Were there a lot?

ACTOR. I don't remember. I suppose so.

NIJINSKY. Was anybody crying?
ACTOR. Of course! I was.
NIJINSKY. Where was all this, by the way?
ACTOR. I think it was in London.
NIJINSKY. Or Paris?
ACTOR. Maybe it was Budapest.
NIJINSKY. But it definitely wasn't in Petersburg, was it?

(Both laugh)

Incidentally, it was in London that they called me the "prima ballerina!"

(Pause)

Why aren't you laughing?
ACTOR. I don't know. What day is it today?
NIJINSKY. Day? You mean, of the week? Yesterday was Tuesday, so that means today is Sunday.
ACTOR. To-day is your birth-day!

(A prolonged pause)

NIJINSKY. Where's my present?
ACTOR. Right here! *(Puts a myrtle wreath around Nijinsky's neck)*
NIJINSKY. Where did you get that?
ACTOR. What's the difference?
NIJINSKY. Where did you get that today is my birthday?
ACTOR. You mean, it isn't?
NIJINSKY. No, I'm happy to… What do you think was in the beginning?
ACTOR. Everybody knows: the word.
NIJINSKY. You see, but it wasn't the word!
ACTOR. What was it, then?
NIJINSKY. A sound. In the beginning was a sound. A strange, unfamiliar, barely discernable sound.
ACTOR. What about dance?
NIJINSKY. Dance… I replaced it.
ACTOR. I see. When a name dies, memories about a person come to life. When a person dies, his name is on everyone's lips. Isn't that so?
NIJINSKY. What did they diagnose you with?
ACTOR. What did who diagnose me with?
NIJINSKY. You know who.
ACTOR. Uh, you know… slowly progressive schizophrenia. What about you?

NIJINSKY. Mine's rapidly progressive. Have you ever tried eating China?

ACTOR. China? N-o. But I devoured America and Europe.

NIJINSKY. All of America?

ACTOR. I didn't leave a crumb.

NIJINSKY. Well, I ate Mongolia. "Hello, how are you feeling?" The main thing is to let them think you are an egoist. Only don't accept any medications!

ACTOR. I can get out of here any time I want!

(Pause)

NIJINSKY. Well you won't find me when you get back.

ACTOR. I'm not coming back!

NIJINSKY. Don't you understand? They'll bring you back.

ACTOR. Where are you going to be?

NIJINSKY. They're going to take me away.

ACTOR. Will we ever meet again?

NIJINSKY. If we look for each other.

ACTOR. We will look for each other!

NIJINSKY. And maybe we'll even find each other! I know a place to hide.

ACTOR. Where?

NIJINSKY. In rhymes. For example: Love!

ACTOR. Glove!

NIJINSKY. God.

ACTOR. Dog. Now let me. Life!

(They stare at each other)

Oh, all right, all right. Death!

NIJINSKY. Stock Exchange!

(They stare at each other)

ACTOR. Prosperity!

NIJINSKY. Politics!

ACTOR. Penitentiary!

NIJINSKY. Critics!

ACTOR. Theorization!

(Stare at each other)

NIJINSKY. Prostitution!

ACTOR. Revolution!

NIJINSKY. Lean meat!
ACTOR. Leonid Myasin![1]

(The two stare at each other)

NIJINSKY. That doesn't rhyme at all. *(Turns away)*

(Pause)

ACTOR. Well, well. Please do pardon me, my dear Prince Myshkin![2] I've
    done a bad thing. If you want, I'll kiss your hand right now!
NIJINSKY. I would never have thought you were like that! I thought you
    were incapable of confession.
ACTOR. What is it has given me the idea recently that you are an idiot? You
    notice things nobody else notices. One can talk to you, but it's best not to!
NIJINSKY. For some reason, everybody considers me an idiot! It's true I
    once was so sick that I was as helpless as an idiot. But how can I possibly
    be an idiot now, when I am perfectly capable of understanding that others
    consider me an idiot? Huh?
ACTOR. Huh?
NIJINSKY. I come in here and think: "People say I'm an idiot. But I'm
    smart, and they don't suspect that." I often think that.
ACTOR. Pardon me, but with whom am I speaking?
NIJINSKY. Prince Lev Nikolayevich Myshkin, at your service.
ACTOR. You mean, Vaslav Fomych Nijinsky?
NIJINSKY. Who's that?
ACTOR. Repeat!

(Pause)

NIJINSKY. Is this some kind of joke?

(Pause)

ACTOR. I don't get you…
NIJINSKY. Is today really my birthday?

---

[1]Leonid Myasin (1895–1979), whose last name is very similar to the Russian word
for meat—"myaso"—was the dancer who replaced Nijinsky in the Ballets Russes in
1919. He went on to a long, brilliant career as a dancer, choreographer and artistic
director.

[2]Prince Lev Nikolayevich Myshkin is the main character of Fyodor Dostoevsky's
novel, *The Idiot*. Myshkin is considered an idiot in society because he is the nearly-
perfect human, a Christ-like figure.

(Pause)

ACTOR. Really. Congratulations.

NIJINSKY. Thank you. I spent my favorite birthday with Chaplin. We talked about his mother. He loved her very tenderly.

ACTOR. But you don't speak English!

NIJINSKY. Yes, nor he Russian.

(Pause)

ACTOR. What do you love most of all on earth?

NIJINSKY. Most of all on earth? *(Laughs)* Insects and parrots.

ACTOR. Unfortunately, I don't like either one. What do you hate?

NIJINSKY. Ringing telephones.

ACTOR. Your ideal?

NIJINSKY. Nietzsche.

ACTOR. Your favorite object?

NIJINSKY. A mirror… no, wait. Yes, a mirror.

ACTOR. Your most treasured dream?

NIJINSKY. To see the light.

ACTOR. In what sense.

NIJINSKY. Next question!

ACTOR. What thought has pursued you all life long?

NIJINSKY. You mean, like an idée fixe?

ACTOR. *(Startled)* Yeah, sort of.

NIJINSKY. A circle. Not a square, but a circle. Like an eye. The theater must be like that, you know?

ACTOR. Uhuh. Do you believe dreams?

NIJINSKY. I don't believe life!

ACTOR. Do you believe dreams?

NIJINSKY. Not all of them.

ACTOR. Favorite flower?

NIJINSKY. Narcissus.

ACTOR. Don't lie.

NIJINSKY. Rose.

ACTOR. Don't lie!

NIJINSKY. Narcissus!

ACTOR. All right. Color?

NIJINSKY. Coffee.

ACTOR. Me too! Smell?

NIJINSKY. Backstage.

ACTOR. I can't stand it! Season?

NIJINSKY. *(Falls into thought)* I am not sufficiently prepared to answer that question. Winter in Europe.

ACTOR. Winter in Europe. Favorite dish?

NIJINSKY. Aren't you going to ask about my favorite breed of dog?

ACTOR. No.

NIJINSKY. Pomegranate.

ACTOR. That's not a dish!

NIJINSKY. Then what is it?

ACTOR. *(Offended)* It's just a fruit.

NIJINSKY. Sometimes you are completely unbearable. It's impossible to talk to you!

(Pause)

Why so silent?

(The Actor mutters something)

Oh, all right. A pomegranate is just a fruit. Are you happy, now? Although it's not true. Happy birthday!

(He hangs the wreath around the Actor's neck)

ACTOR. What do you mean?

NIJINSKY. Happy birthday to us both! Congratulations.

ACTOR. Ha! Thanks. What can you tell me about the ballet?

NIJINSKY. Which one?

ACTOR. Any one.

NIJINSKY. Nothing.

ACTOR. Happy birthday! Why so capricious?

NIJINSKY. I don't know what to say. Thanks. Give me a hint!

ACTOR. Let's say, plot, choreography.

NIJINSKY. Oh, plot! It's always the same. "What's the plot of your story?" There is none.

(The Actor laughs)

That's right. You've either got to have a plot that nobody knows at all or that everybody everywhere knows. It's like looking at a painting or listening to a symphony. For example, I could devise a dance for a hunchback, could you?

ACTOR. Me? No!

NIJINSKY. There, you see? You just waved me off with your hand. That was an expressive gesture. Choreography makes use of the very same gesture, only in an artificially created environment. That's all there is to it. What's it to you?

ACTOR. I heard something about the ballet once. But I don't remember it now! Something about a pretty castle.

NIJINSKY. Yes! The castle of beauty. Yeah. That's not bad. It's only a game, of course. But I know one thing, there is no such thing as a dance that is independent from death.

ACTOR. *(Tossing off the wreath)* No such thing as a dance that is independent from death? *(Pause)* What about this? *(Does a rock 'n' roll dance)*

(Nijinsky laughs)

Say, how was it that you could hang in the air at the top of a leap?

NIJINSKY. That's simple. You just get a bit of a running start, take off, and then, for a minute, you just stop in the air.

ACTOR. *(Stopping)* What do you mean, just stop?

NIJINSKY. It's easy. Try it.

ACTOR. Me? Come on! I don't have any experience.

NIJINSKY. So what? All experience does is kill a good leap. Come on, come on! Go over there to that curtain.

ACTOR. What are you doing? It won't work.

NIJINSKY. You need room to build up speed. Go on over there. The most important thing is to think of nothing. Absolutely nothing.

ACTOR. Cut it out! This is crazy!

NIJINSKY. Don't worry!

ACTOR. What's the point? This is stupid!

NIJINSKY. Try it. Just try it. O.k., right here. You start running and... I'll stand right where you should start your leap.

(Pause. The Actor prepares to leap)

ACTOR. Uh, when should I start?

NIJINSKY. *(Thinking)* As soon as you're ready, I'll wave my hand. *(Pause)*

ACTOR. *(Walking away)* This is pointless. Plus, I'm afraid of heights.

NIJINSKY. Take your position! Quick! Push off from where I'm standing. Ready? Go!

(Nijinsky waves his hand, the Actor starts running. He leaps and flies into the air. Both carefully watch the trajectory of the Actor's leap and laugh at that moment when they imagine he comes back to earth)

ACTOR. I can't! *(Pause)* I can't do it.

NIJINSKY. No need to get upset. Nobody can do it. I'm probably the only one. You should have seen how the critics ate me alive! They couldn't wait to find a reason to destroy me! Just think. An artist devotes his entire life to art and the critics—even if they aren't prejudiced—don't think twice about moving in to destroy him.

ACTOR. Ha! They think they're smarter than actors. They like making the poor devils shiver and tremble.

NIJINSKY. What did you say? Poor devils? That's exactly right. I've got to write that down.

ACTOR. To listen to critics, you'd think that without them there is no such thing as art and that no one had the right to express an opinion about anything without getting their approval first!

NIJINSKY. That's why I never paid any attention to critics!

ACTOR. I guess their... work, that they get money for, requires a certain, uh, diligence. But it doesn't have anything to do with love of art!

NIJINSKY. Love?! What love?! They don't do anything but theorize!

ACTOR. You know, all this time I've been wanting to ask you...

NIJINSKY. About what?

ACTOR. About, you know, the most important thing.

NIJINSKY. Well, go ahead. Ask me!

ACTOR. I forgot everything!

NIJINSKY. Try to remember.

ACTOR. (Shaking his head) I forget. I forgot everything.

NIJINSKY. I'll be happy to answer. What was it you wanted to know?

ACTOR. I don't remember.

NIJINSKY. But isn't that why you're still here?

ACTOR. Maybe. It doesn't matter now.

NIJINSKY. Freeze!

(The Actor freezes)

NIJINSKY. From here you look just like me.

ACTOR. From where?

NIJINSKY. Come here!

(The Actor goes to Nijinsky)

From right here!

ACTOR. But I'm not there.

NIJINSKY. What do you mean? You mean, you can't see? There was even a photograph where I looked just like that. And now you are all illuminated, too!

(The Actor stares harder. Pause)

ACTOR. I see. No I don't. No, I see it. No I don't. This is stupid! What do you keep harassing me for? Now you see it, now you don't! Are you satisfied now? How did this happen to me? Somehow I got mixed up in something incredibly absurd! What kind of rules are you playing by? And here I am like a fool playing along! This is dis-gus-ting. You hooked me, you pathetic slob! *(Laughs)* Here I am playing this humiliating role! For who? The "prima ballerina!" Ah! *(Pause)* By the way, one sick weirdo like you said that the word God stands for Galactic Organizational Director *(Laughs)* I thinks that's more clever than all your nonsense about God!

(Long pause)

NIJINSKY. When I was a boy…
ACTOR. Shut up.
NIJINSKY. I used to copy out Pushkin's poems, hoping I would learn to write like he did. Something like, "I'm sitting on pins in a dungeon so damp…"[3]
ACTOR. "God grant I don't go nuts."
NIJINSKY. That's right! I wrote several poems myself, but nobody, nobody ever read them.
ACTOR. No wonder! What rhymes with "existence"?
NIJINSKY. Nijinsky.
ACTOR. What?
NIJINSKY. Vaslav Nijinsky.
ACTOR. Again!
NIJINSKY. Nijinsky. What was in the beginning?

ACTOR.
In the beginning was a sound. An unfamiliar one.
A hum. And then came lines of letters.
I slept. And swarms of hands traced out a word. I've lost it now.
I woke and saw a pitch-black door and nothing more.
An uninvited guest then joined the agonizing native
Of that undesired night that was so tender!
Merciless life, that unforgiving tempter,
Flew into a madhouse with a leap,
And for a moment stopped being mere life,
Transforming into something more! My soul—which no one can
Humiliate—spinning like a bright snowflake,
Is ready to do servitude!
It waits its future incarnation with impatience!

---

[3]Nijinsky rephrases the first line of Pushkin's poem, "The Prisoner." The original translates literally as, "I sit behind bars in a damp dungeon."

NIJINSKY.
  You speak? He speaks! It can't be true!
  That's not the outcome I was working to!
  And it's your fault. You are the one who lacked
  The love that would have gained you loss…
  It's nothing but a sleight of hand —
  He cannot change. I don't believe he can!
  Oh, as I played, I tightly drew the knot.
  Don't delay! The move is yours! Your shot!

(Pause)

ACTOR. There's a plot for you! Who could have guessed it would…
NIJINSKY. *(Interrupting)* It's the resolution. The finale.
ACTOR. But we're absolutely out of time. Whose resolution?
NIJINSKY. The only one possible. The time has come.
ACTOR. Yes, the time has come to finish with this… visit.
NIJINSKY. Well then?

(Pause)

ACTOR. Agreed.

(Pause)

NIJINSKY. All right. *(Takes out two pistols and loads them)* Antiques. They are
  quite reliable.
ACTOR. I do hope and willingly trust that's so.
NIJINSKY. The choice, sir, is yours.
ACTOR. What's the difference? However, I'll take this one.
NIJINSKY. This?
ACTOR. Yes. It better suits my attire.
NIJINSKY. That remains to be seen.
ACTOR. Naturally. Undoubtedly. Well? Shall we? How many paces?
NIJINSKY. How many is the usual? I must admit, I am not well versed in
  the arithmetics of duels. How many did Lermontov use?
ACTOR. It seems I've danced a duel or two… Let's just say ten. *(Goes to
  measure out the paces and establish the barrier)*
NIJINSKY. *(Takes out money)* I do not wish to remain in your debt. *(Throws
  the packet of money at the Actor)*
ACTOR. What a shame you never made it to Paris or to Zurich.
NIJINSKY. *(Pointing to the wreath)* By the way, you were wrong. Today is not
  my birthday.

(Pause)

ACTOR. Would the gentleman care to be my second?

NIJINSKY. I see no other choice. And in turn, good sir, if it wouldn't be too much trouble…

ACTOR. My goodness, no! I would be pleased and honored. And now, what about a doctor?

NIJINSKY. I think that is unnecessary.

ACTOR. But it is tradition!

NIJINSKY. I can take on that function myself.

ACTOR. Won't that be a bit much for one person?

NIJINSKY. Not at all. Don't you worry!

ACTOR. As an honorable second, I am obliged to offer a peaceful settlement. Perhaps the gentlemen will apologize to one another and shake hands?

NIJINSKY. And then what? *(Pause)* I have nothing to apologize for.

ACTOR. That goes doubly for me.

NIJINSKY. Then, let's dispense with the formalities!

ACTOR. Yes. Let's dispense with these horrid clichés. Are you ready?

NIJINSKY. Sir! We forgot to determine whose shot shall be the first!

ACTOR. One moment! *(Takes out a coin)*

(Nijinsky approaches)

Heads or tails?

NIJINSKY. Call it tails or nothing.

ACTOR. Tails it is. We shall see who is the prince and who's the pauper! *(He flips the coin)* He laughs best who shoots last. *(Looks at the coin)* It's heads.

NIJINSKY. You, sir, are having uncommon luck.

ACTOR. Shall we take our places?

NIJINSKY. Yes. It would be silly to shoot at the distance of a single pace.

ACTOR. Why does sir say that?

NIJINSKY. Sir says that because if there were nothing to separate us at all, then what would be the point of dueling?

(Pause)

ACTOR. I see your point! How is your eyesight?

NIJINSKY. Better than yours.

ACTOR. We shall see.

NIJINSKY. Enough dallying! To our places!

ACTOR. As regards your reference to the passage of time, I heartily agree. However, I dare note that our place is one and the same.

NIJINSKY. Depends on your point of view!

(Nijinsky goes to one side of the stage, and then suddenly whirls around and goes to the other. They separate. The stage is empty. Pause. From offstage the Actor's voice is heard: "Begin!" They begin walking toward each other. Nijinsky lowers his pistol)

ACTOR. What's the matter?

NIJINSKY. Just look at yourself! You can't go fighting a duel in such filthy shoes! *(Takes out a pair of shoes)* Try these on.

(The Actor puts on the shoes)

Excellent! A perfect fit! I'd be happy to give them to you, but now is not the time for gifts.

ACTOR. Thank you.

(They separate.)

Hey! You forgot your pistol!

(Nijinsky returns and takes his pistol. They separate again. Pause. The Actor's voice is heard: "Begin!" They walk toward each other)

I have the feeling my pistol isn't loaded.

NIJINSKY. That's impossible. I loaded both of them.

ACTOR. In your haste you might have forgotten one.

NIJINSKY. Who's the one who showed up with an empty suitcase?

(They stare at one another)

ACTOR. I'll check. *(He checks his pistol)*

NIJINSKY. To our places!

(They separate. The Actor shouts: "Hut!" Nijinsky answers: "What do you mean, 'hut'? This isn't a circus act. Begin!" They approach one another. A telephone rings. The duelists freeze)

NIJINSKY. You get it. And tell them I'm not here, nor will I be.

ACTOR. Why me? Maybe we just shouldn't answer?

NIJINSKY. Then I won't be able to concentrate on you!

ACTOR. *(Approaches the telephone)* All right, we'll call it your last wish. Hello? Hello? Speak up! *(Slams down the receiver)* For the love of God!